CREATING
PASSION-DRIVEN
TEAMS

How to Stop Micromanaging
and
Motivate People to Top Performance

CREATING
PASSION-DRIVEN
TEAMS

How to Stop Micromanaging
and
Motivate People to Top Performance

By

DAN BOBINSKI

CAREER
PRESS

This edition first published in 2009 by Career Press, an imprint of
Red Wheel/Weiser, LLC
With offices at:
65 Parker Street, Suite 7
Newburyport, MA 01950
www.redwheelweiser.com
www.careerpress.com

ISBN: 978-1-60163-075-9

Library of Congress Cataloging-in-Publication Data
Bobinski, Dan.
    Creating passion-driven teams : how to stop micromanaging and
motivate people to top performance / by Dan Bobinski.
        p. cm.
    Includes index.
    ISBN 978-1-60163-075-9
    1. Teams in the workplace. 2. Employee motivation. I. Title.

HD66.B623 2009
658.4'022--dc22

                                                    2009004581

Cover design by Rob Johnson, Johnson Designs

Printed in the United States of America
IBI
10 9 8 7 6 5 4 3 2 1

To all who see
the grand possibilities,
and
believe in their heart.

Acknowledgments

So many people helped with this project in so many ways. Here I thank just a few, alphabetically, of course.

Thank you to Giles Anderson, without whose brainstorming, guidance, advice, and initiative, this project would have never even started. To John L.V. Bobell, for pressing me when pressing was needed. To Eugene Bobinski, I'm really glad you're my dad. To Elsieanne Cook, your unselfish hours made such a difference. To Robert Croker, who is "always there." To Jim Grove, for disciplining my pen. To Michael Kroth, an extraordinary idea man and encourager. To Norris Krueger, may your wit and wisdom never part. To Ilya Kucherencko, for the great insights. To Nancy Lull, who is not afraid to speak her mind…at all. To Jim Medina, I probably couldn't have kept my head straight without your help. To Kathleen Morris, for setting it up and all the support. To Debra Murray, for the realism and business insight. To Kelly Pound, for being a phenomenal support, friend, and encourager. To Lorena Roberts, for the years of being there while this book percolated. For Greg Sigerson, for brainstorming, encouraging, brainstorming, encouraging, and also for encouraging. To Rose Sulfridge, for reminding me about grammar. To Michael Tomlin, the pro, for your uncanny way of making me think. To Kim Weber, for your frank honesty when frank honesty was needed. To the Beginning and the End. You know why. Thank you all.

Contents

Foreword

At a recent conference of economic developers, the following statement jolted me: "We are fifty years into the Information Age, and we are still managing like we are in the Industrial Age."

Based on my interactions with thousands of businesses, I believe this statement is absolutely true, and most leaders don't know where to start.

Dan Bobinski's *Creating Passion-Driven Teams* helps bring focus to the most critical area in today's Information Age business world: people.

In the Information Age, we have shifted to an economy that is much more driven by services. A service-based economy's primary assets are people and their innate ability to identify and solve problems—to innovate with purpose. In this "how-to" book, Dan highlights the almost unlimited upside to unlocking the potential of individuals and teams working toward common goals.

When reading a book, I first peruse the table of contents to get a sense of what is covered. When looking at the table of contents in this book, my first reaction was "this looks like a bunch of familiar topics." However, when I started reading, I found myself drinking deeply from Dan's principles and examples, and realizing how far I had to go to provide the kind of environment that enables and unlocks the capability of the people around me—and even within myself.

I whole heartedly recommend *Creating Passion-Driven Teams*. For some, it will be an eye-opener to things you have not really thought about. For others, it will provide a much-needed reminder of things you say you believe in, but aren't doing. Either way, the practices Dan describes need to become habits for all of us, as they are necessary to create the type of teams needed for success in today's business world.

—Gary Harpst,
Veteran CEO and best-selling author of
Six Disciplines Execution Revolution

Introduction

Passion-Driven Teams.
Just what is a passion-driven team? Relying on my trusty dictionary, here's my interpretation:

> *A cooperative group of people linked in common purpose (who are) forcibly compelled toward an activity that they like, that they find important, and in which they invest time and energy.*

Wow. Who wouldn't want to be on a team like that? The one question that needs answering is "Where is the compelling force?" The answer to that question has been elusive for many managers.

After 20-plus years as a business owner, trainer, consultant, executive coach, keynote speaker, and columnist, and with all of my work revolving around workplace issues and having worked with executives and leadership teams in Fortune 500 companies, as well as owners and management teams in small and mid-sized companies, I've come to a few conclusions about that compelling force:

1. It can't be manufactured.
2. It can't be demanded.
3. It can't be bought.
4. It can't be faked.

The elusive force—passion—must *emerge*.

For the person who serves on a team and sees the grand possibilities of that team being compelled by passion, this book is for you. It is a noble desire. Stay the course.

If you seek to create a team driven by passion, then you must look within each person on your team, for it's there that the passion resides. As I said, it cannot be manufactured, demanded, bought, or faked. It must come out by invitation of the person who owns it. Each person must release it.

And here lies the heart of this book: If you want to create passion-driven teams, the only thing you can do is create the conditions in which the people on your team feel safe enough to release their treasured passion. In other words:

➤ When enough trust exists, it becomes possible.

➤ When enough belief exists, it becomes possible.

➤ When enough sharing exists, it becomes possible.

➤ When enough camaraderie exists, it becomes possible.

➤ When enough commitment exists, it becomes possible.

➤ When enough common purpose exists, it becomes possible.

➤ When enough determined confidence exists, it becomes possible.

But on a team, when passion is ready to fully emerge, it must be released by all.

As I said, your endeavor to create a passion-driven team is a noble one, and should be pursued. This book was written to give you insights I've gained throughout the past 20-plus years on how to create the conditions in which passion-driven teams can emerge.

When I've seen passion-driven teams, they had caring people at the helm, and people who cared throughout the team (Chapter 1). All team members knew their roles and responsibilities (Chapter 2). They knew what caused micromanagement, and they knew how to steer clear of it (Chapters 3 and 4). They understood each other very, very well (Chapter 5) and didn't play head games (Chapter 6).

The people I've observed on passion-driven teams were can-do thinkers (Chapter 7), understood how to work together effectively to get things done (Chapter 8), and stayed in balance (Chapter 9).

They listened carefully to each other (Chapter 10) and quickly resolved any disagreements that arose (Chapter 11).

They acquired whatever skills they needed to succeed (Chapter 12), and if ever they fell down, they got right back up again (Chapter 13). And they guarded their crowning achievements very carefully (Chapter 14), celebrating the rare thing that they had: a *Passion-Driven Team.*

Chapter 1

Are You a Builder or a Climber?

The fact that you're holding this book right now tells me you want to make a difference in the world, your industry, or maybe just where you work. It could be you're a leader wanting to elevate your teams to a whole new level. Perhaps you're an experienced manager or team leader and you'd like your teams to be more effective and vibrant. Maybe you've just been promoted and you want to get a jump on things so you can hit the ground running. Or maybe you're a front-line employee who wants to develop your capacity for teambuilding.

Whatever your role, if you want to make a difference, you probably realize the value of having teams that are passionate. We love seeing teams flow with energy and enthusiasm, getting past obstacles, and achieving their goals with unshakable confidence.

Unfortunately, we also know that the chances of teams becoming that way on their own are pretty slim. The conditions for it have to be right.

Although a "teaming" revival has been zinging around the globe for several decades now, the concept of teams has been around since our ancestors worked together to hunt mammoths. Yet despite the recent increased focus, most teams today are nowhere near as effective as they could be. The reasons are many: lack of structure, lack of communication, and lack of well-defined roles and responsibilities, to name a few. But one reason overrides all the rest: a lack of passion.

Passion may be the most powerful factor in teams reaching the highest levels of performance. A passion-driven team operates with an unwavering confidence. Team members act responsibly, but believe they can accomplish any task set before them. Each person has internalized the team's vision, mission, and values, creating an unbreakable camaraderie with "commitment to the cause." They love to learn, get and give feedback, and share their experiences and resources for the betterment of the team.

But how do we get teams to be passionate?

Teams are comprised of people, not things. Therefore, to create a passion-driven team, the person leading that team must understand how people tend to respond in various environments. He or she must know what conditions attract and energize people, and what leads them to crave eager involvement. He or she also must know what conditions people find objectionable, leading them to disengage or withdraw their involvement altogether.

Creating Conditions for Passion

We cannot force people to become passionate. A team leader must create the right conditions for passion to emerge. Those conditions must be nurtured or tended to, not unlike a gardener creating the right conditions for his plants to flourish.

Think about it; gardeners don't make plants grow—the genetic coding inside each plant does that. A gardener simply creates conditions that are conducive to plant growth. If those conditions are maintained, then growth occurs.

A conscientious gardener frequently evaluates the conditions of the garden. Is fertilizer needed? More water? Less water? Are there any unwanted pests or diseases?

Gardeners ask these types of questions and make adjustments as needed, because they know what kind of results they'll get if they simply give a plant an intimidating look and bark out a command to "grow!"

Likewise, to get the best results in the workplace, managers and team leaders should be inquisitive about the conditions of their teams and the preferences of the people on them. Unfortunately, many managers bark out "grow" commands to their teams and blame the workers if no growth occurs.

What's strange is that we tolerate such behavior in managers, but we'd laugh if a gardener acted that way.

If gardening is not something to which you relate, let's use another analogy. A carpenter does not look at a blueprint and then bark out an order for the wood to shape itself accordingly. Good carpenters know the characteristics of different woods, and recognize that each project requires selecting a wood appropriate for the job. For example, wood that is excellent for fireplace mantels or outdoor furniture may not be the same wood chosen for making bowls, cabinets, or lamps.

Carpenters also know the capabilities of their tools—which tools enable them to shape wood the way they want it, and when to use each one. For example, they know when a hand sander is needed instead of a belt-sander, and when using a band saw is more appropriate than a scroll saw.

For every job, a carpenter plans ahead to determine what pieces of wood and which tools he will use to create the best possible end-product.

My point is that thriving gardens and quality woodwork do not simply appear. People striving for the best in these professions become ardent students of their craft. Any manager or team leader striving to create passion-driven teams must do the same.

Becoming a student

Consider Cynthia, an engineer at a large high-tech company. Out of her own pocket she paid a management coach so she could learn what she knew she didn't know about teambuilding. She read as many books as she could on the subject, and talked with people she considered to be successful managers of teams so she could hear "the voice of experience."

Alongside Cynthia was a coworker named Tom, a hotshot engineer whose skills earned the respect of many. Tom believed his natural skills would be his ticket up the corporate ladder. Imagine his surprise when six months later, Cynthia was promoted to a management position. Later, when Cynthia was further promoted into a director's position, Tom was in the same position, wondering why he hadn't received any promotions.

Unfortunately, many managers and team leaders don't realize what Cynthia realized: To build passion-driven teams, one must learn the skills necessary to create passion-driven teams. Furthermore, such learning does not happen overnight. As we will see, people on passion-driven teams embrace an attitude of lifelong learning. It only makes sense that the leaders of such teams set the pace and do the same.

Becoming a student of creating and sustaining passion-driven teams involves drawing from many resources. This book is one of them. Many other books will also be helpful (see the Appendix on page 199), as will newsletters, magazines, and online sources that delve into best practices on teambuilding.

You may also want to enlist the help of a management coach, and perhaps even form your own mastermind group to brainstorm ideas and get feedback from like-minded peers.

The point is that you must become a student of people; you have to study their dreams, fears, aspirations, and hopes, and learn to create the conditions in which people come together for a common purpose. After all, creating passion-driven teams requires a new level of thinking.

Think about the number of managers and team leaders whose teams are fragmented or simply surviving. Too often, managers and team leaders believe they've been placed in those positions because of their natural style—not in spite of it.

What's Your Style?

It seems that dozens of different styles have been identified in recent decades. Leaders and managers have been recognized as charismatic, bureaucratic, Machiavellian, democratic, authoritarian, and laissez-faire.

We also have micromanagers, coaches, and servant leaders. The list goes on, but there's a thread or attribute that runs through every management and leadership style, and it involves how people interact with and value the people around them.

To help us understand this attribute, we can view it as a spectrum. At one end of the spectrum are Builders, at the other end are Climbers. Every person has a tendency to operate at a particular point on the spectrum, and it's natural to move one way or the other as a situation warrants. Realize that where we operate is a choice. You are not locked in. Every person is free to choose how they interact with and value others.

However, I must emphasize that where you operate on this spectrum and how you weave this thread into your personal leadership style may be the largest factor in determining your ability to create passion-driven teams. The overwhelming majority of the time it is Builders that have the most success in this effort; Climbers rarely do.

Let's take a closer look at how Builders and Climbers affect the workplace.

Builders and Climbers

People on the Builder side of the spectrum devote their efforts to building up the people in their organization. They help others improve upon or gain new skills. They mentor, they coach, and they keep the blueprints in mind (the organization's mission, vision, values, and strategies), using them as a guide for deciding what direction to take for learning, and how to help both themselves and other team members grow.

Like good craftsmen, Builders keep an eye on quality, because they know when they retire or leave the organization, the condition of the people who were on their teams will be a direct reflection of them.

At the other end of the spectrum are Climbers. They also want the organization to succeed, but are firm believers in the "sink or swim" approach. Along those lines, they believe that if you fall in the pool, it's your own responsibility to climb out.

Climbers are mainly concerned about achieving their own personal goals, and may climb over other people to reach them. They'll look at the blueprints (the vision, mission, values, and strategies), but too often it's only to determine where they can climb next. Climbers adopt an attitude that if you want something, you should be able to figure it out how to get it on your own.

A tale of two managers

Enthusiasm in the workplace diminishes when Climbers get placed in charge of teams. To illustrate, let's introduce Gary, a senior production manager in a Midwest manufacturing plant. He worked his way into that position using a rough, abrasive, intimidating style. He threatened people with their jobs. He got angry and raised his voice often. Essentially, in his quest to be the can-do superstar, he pushed each team to the end of its rope. In Gary's mind, his teams were weak and they needed his strength to get the results that were expected. That thinking paid off for Gary—he rose through the ranks just like he wanted.

Yet, as you might surmise, the result of Gary's style was teams motivated by fear, not passion. Fear-based motivation does not last, so Gary needed an increasing amount of fear and intimidation just to maintain his production numbers.

You can imagine what eventually happened. Morale went through the floor, people started calling in sick, and complaints were filed. But, similar to an inexperienced gardener who believes the best way to treat sick plants is to simply give them more water, sunlight, or fertilizer, Gary pressed his team even harder with increased levels of intimidation.

After all, he couldn't let up. He believed that pressing his people to higher levels of production would land him on the next rung of the corporate ladder.

Jeff was another senior production manager at the same company as Gary, but he favored a different approach. Jeff was known as a listener. He asked for input from his team members, and he gave them plenty of feedback to keep them informed about what was going on. He also made sure people got cross-trained in areas that interested them, as well as in the critical positions.

Perhaps most important, Jeff was fair. He never shied away from correcting people if mistakes were made, and discipline was always handled tactfully. When an employee left Jeff's office after being corrected, he or she always felt valued and respected.

Obviously, when it comes to how they interact with and value people, Gary is a Climber, and Jeff is a Builder. Gary believes he must push people toward the end result, while Jeff has learned that results are much easier to achieve when people are valued, trained, and mentored. He knows people's passions get engaged when they feel included.

Every action has ripple effects

Let's also consider another Climber and the ripple effects of her actions. Marsha was the general manager for a small group of newspapers that was acquired by a larger media conglomerate. The sales manager who reported to Marsha was a client of mine and told me the following story:

In our industry we have three types of accounts—local, regional, and national. As the sales manager, my book of business included the regional and national accounts as well as a few local ones. The money from regional and national accounts made up between 15 and 30 thousand dollars of my monthly numbers, from which I earned a 10 percent commission.

When we were bought out, Marsha told me the regional and national accounts would be house accounts from that point forward, and that she would be handling them. I was told the switch was to accommodate a policy held by the new owners.

The immediate ripple effect was less time to spend with my sales people as I hit the streets trying to compensate for lost income. After six months, my team was struggling. We were consistently 10 to 15 thousand under goal, and Marsha's new boss decided I wasn't cutting it as a sales manager. Without any warning, I was let go.

A few months later I bumped into a person from the newspaper and we took the opportunity to catch up over lunch. What I found out shocked me.

It turns out that when the company was purchased, Marsha's main goal was keeping her job. She knew she could do that as long as she met the bottom line numbers set forth by the new owners. By taking over the regional and national accounts, she didn't have to pay anyone a commission, and that added an instant $1,500–$3,000 to her bottom line.

But I also learned that Marsha used those accounts as a slush fund to keep the books in the black each month. If we'd had a good month, she'd hide some income from those accounts. And if a month was looking thin, she'd tack on some of the money she'd previously hidden. Apparently, the new owners didn't scrutinize the books that closely. Their only concern was the bottom line, and Marsha made sure she always met that number.

Obviously she didn't care about me or my sales team. For Marsha, it was all about keeping her job.

Are You a Builder or a Climber?

Teams can have problems when they have Climbers who think they are Builders. This happens when Climbers rationalize that their actions are helping the team meet its goals. Unfortunately, this misguided self-diagnosis is fairly common. For example, when teaching this material to a group of C-level executives from a private corporation, I wasn't surprised when each person identified him- or herself as a Builder.

A few months later, when I was working with the next level of managers in that same organization, they, too, proclaimed themselves to be Builders. But when I asked them about the C-level executives above them, all I heard was "Oh my—they are all Climbers!"

That pattern repeated itself with every group of managers that came through the training. Each group saw themselves as Builders, with those higher on the organizational chart usually described as Climbers. Whether this was a genuine lack of self-awareness among the managers or a misperception among those lower on the organizational chart, this pattern persisted throughout the organization.

Because the only person we have 100 percent control over is ourselves, might I suggest that each of us stop and look within? A self-assessment is in order.

Self-Assessment: Builder or Climber?

The following self-confrontation questions can give us a clearer view of reality. Although these are simple yes or no questions, be deeply honest with yourself. For example, your answer to a question might be "yes" 40 percent of the time, but that means your answer is "no" 60 percent of the time. (To get an unbiased glimpse at the truth, ask people who have no vested interest in your ego to answer these questions about you!)

1. Do you encourage and help other people to work toward the same professional growth activities that you choose for yourself?

2. Do you sacrifice your time in the spotlight to train others to be better at what they do?

3. Do you ask for help on projects and share the credit when accolades come?

4. Do you truly enjoy giving a boost to someone's self-esteem?

5. Do you prioritize looking for ways to solve problems instead of looking for someone to blame?

6. When someone comes to you with a problem, do you listen more than talk?

7. Do you share new knowledge and information with those around you?

8. Do you look for ways to help others be better at what they do?

9. When things go wrong, do you take responsibility as quickly and to the same degree as you take credit when things go right?

10. When you do something for others, is it done without expectation of something in return?

If you can answer yes to these questions, chances are you operate as a Builder. This means that your chosen manner of valuing other people increases your likelihood of success when creating passion-driven teams.

If you can answer yes to most, but not all, that's a good sign, but you may have a few tendencies that inhibit passion on your teams.

If you answer no to most or all of these questions, chances are you operate as a Climber and you are unaware of the negative impact you have on the people within your organization. It's been my experience that many Climbers sincerely want to become Builders and genuinely contribute to a cause bigger than themselves.

If that's you, revisiting the 10 questions and looking for ways to improve is as good a place to start as any. Of course, I'd also recommend becoming a student of the material in this book. You can also visit *www.passiondriventeams.com* and read more about becoming a Builder.

However, if you've discovered you operate as a Climber, but you don't want to become a Builder, I recommend putting this book down to avoid wasting your time. Facts are facts: Passion-driven teams consist of people who invest in each other. Climbers who try to force passion into place may experience occasional or partial success in teambuilding, but the thin veil eventually falls off. People operating as Climbers do not have a good track record for creating passion-driven teams.

Remember Jeff, our senior production manager who managed people with a Builder mentality? He wound up being promoted, and I've recently been told he's being groomed for an executive position. Gary, the man who operated as a Climber, was passed over for a promotion several times and remains a senior production manager. Fortunately, he's come to realize that he needs to do things differently, and he's addressing the issue.

What You Need to Get Started

Okay, either you've discovered you operate as a Builder, or you realize you've been a Climber and you want to change that. The rest of this book gives you a set of guidelines for creating the conditions that top managers and team leaders use to create passion-driven teams. But there's one more thing. You'll need to make a few commitments:

➤ A commitment to personal and professional growth within yourself.

➤ A commitment to stick to the principles and practices of being a Builder, and not give up if things don't fall into place in the given timeline.

➤ A commitment to become a student of the people on your team. Just like plants and different types of wood, each person is unique. Conditions that create growth in one plant may hinder it in another. You must commit to being a perpetual student of people.

The bottom line is that you can't shortchange the process for creating passion-driven teams, as shortcuts in such efforts always fail. Granted, shortcuts may produce short-term results, but I guarantee that a consistent long-term effort will give you much better results than intermittent short bursts of energy that must be continually re-ignited.

Commit to being a Builder of people, and you have the foundation for creating passion-driven teams.

Chapter 2

The Management Matrix

Perhaps you've been on a team where roles and responsibilities were unclear or misunderstood. If so, you probably experienced doubt, confusion, and frustration, all of which eat away at the energy of passion. Think of a relay team: four runners, each running one lap with a baton getting passed from runner to runner. If even one person is unclear of his or her role or responsibilities, it creates conditions that inhibit the flow of passion for the entire team.

This problem can be especially dangerous in the workplace, where the absence of clearly defined roles and responsibilities can go unnoticed for years. How does that happen? Most often it's because people want to be productive, so they find ways to stay busy and make valuable contributions to the organization's goals. They may not be functioning in their proper role nor performing their most vital duties, but they stay industrious with contributions that make a difference. It's hard to notice if people need redirection to perform their core responsibilities (and can be even harder for us to actually re-direct them) when they are giving 100 percent, especially if what they're doing produces seemingly reasonable results.

This problem just gets worse when people get moved into a team leader's role or receive a promotion, and receive very little training for understanding how their new position contributes to the big picture.

Key Roles and Core Responsibilities

For teams to function at their best, people must be aware of three basic roles common to almost every organization.

Your success in creating passion-driven teams will be helped by understanding a very simple matrix that describes the responsibilities for each of these three roles.

Let's start with clarifying the roles. Then we'll boil down the stereotypical organizational chart to three basic levels in a way that illustrates the core responsibilities. First the roles:

1. *Leadership.* This is the top of the organizational chart, and includes positions such as owners, presidents, vice presidents, school superintendents, and C-level officers.

2. *Management.* Includes lead workers, supervisors, front line managers, team leaders, middle managers, school principals, and department heads.

3. *Front-line employees.* Includes everyone from new employees at the entry level to experienced workers in non-supervisory roles.

Obviously, organizations are usually more complex, but for our purposes this simple outline is sufficient.

	What someone is given/placed in charge of	What someone does with what they're given	The expected result of working with the raw product through the process
Leadership	Ideas	Communicate ideas / Seek and consider feedback	Effective organization
	The horizon	Make adjustments	
	Organizational capabilities	Enable and advance organizational capabilities	
Management	Front-line employees	Train the front line	Efficient operations
	Systems used to process raw product	Coordinate with others to improve the systems	
Front Line	Raw product	Process	Outcome

A fresh look at core responsibilities

A few years ago, while giving a keynote address to a group of senior executives, I asked how many of them started their careers in an entry-level position. Naturally, there was a sea of hands.

I asked a few people to describe their first jobs. One gentleman said he had a paper route, delivering newspapers from his bicycle. He told us how he would go to the agency, get the correct number of papers for his route, fold the papers, put a rubber band on them, and then fit them into bags and baskets on his bike before heading out to deliver them.

I pointed out that every job has what we could call "raw product." For his job, the raw product was newspapers, rubber bands, carrying bags, and his bicycle. He nodded.

Then I said that every job also involves a "process." For him it was counting the papers, folding them, arranging them in the bike's basket, and then riding through the neighborhood delivering newspapers to his customers. Again he nodded.

"And what was the outcome of your efforts?" I asked. He responded "People who subscribed to the paper got it delivered to their home."

Another executive said her first job was working in the kitchen of a restaurant. After she described what she did, I summarized: Her "raw product" was not only the meat, the potatoes, the vegetables, but also the pots and pans, the knives, the grill, and so on. The audience nodded.

Then I noted that her "process" was keeping her pots, pans, and grill ready, plus cooking the food according to the customer's order, arranging it on a plate so it had a pleasing appearance, and letting the server know it was ready, all in a timely manner.

"What was the outcome?" I asked. Again, the answer was easy: "Each customer received food just as he or she ordered it."

Another executive told us he worked as a landscaper. His "raw product" was the customers' lawns, their shrubs, his mower, edger, rakes, and brooms. His "process" was edging the lawn, cutting the grass, trimming the hedges, and bagging up all the trimmings. The outcome of his efforts was a neatly manicured lawn.

After a few more examples, everyone saw that each job involves:

A. Some kind of "raw product."

B. A "process" for handling the raw product.

C. A resulting product, which could be called an outcome.

It's a simple formula:

$$A + B = C$$

This formula applies to all jobs, even service industries. For example, if you work in a tax office, the "raw product" is each customer's financial records and the state and federal tax codes. The "process" is filling out the tax forms in keeping with the state and federal codes, so the customer realizes either the best possible return or pays the least amount of taxes required by law. The outcome is that each client has a properly completed tax form.

It doesn't matter what job we're talking about, the three basic responsibilities are:

A. What an employee is given or placed in charge of.

B. What a person is supposed to do with the raw product.

C. The expected result of taking the raw product through the process.

Here's how the matrix looks for front-line employees:

	What someone is given / placed in charge of	What someone does with what they're given	The expected result of working with the raw product through the process
Front Line	Raw Product	Process	Outcome
	A +	B =	C

The need to assess and adjust

Before we look at the management level, we need to acknowledge that every outcome has some level of expectation, usually set by the organization's leadership. This expectation is often a blend of quality and quantity, and because of that, people must learn to evaluate, or assess, what they produce. After all, rarely is a person's work 100 percent uniform every day, with zero need to evaluate quality or quantity. Depending on the conditions of the raw product or how well a process is operating, adjustments of some kind are almost always necessary to meet an expected outcome.

Think about those entry-level jobs our executives once held. The newspaper carrier learned that when the papers were thick, he had to fold them differently than on days when the paper was thin. The cook learned to add a bit of water to the pancake batter if it seemed too thick. And our landscaper learned that after a rain, adjustments were needed as to when the grass was cut.

If you think about the work you've done in your own life, you'll recognize that it's nearly impossible to deliver a quality product or service until you've learned the capabilities, limitations, and nuances of your raw product and its processes.

For now, here's how we illustrate assessing and adjusting on the matrix:

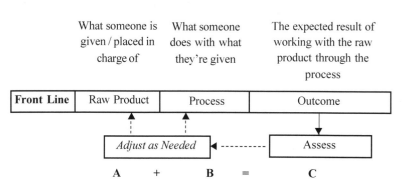

The Management Level

The joy in this model is that the formula (A + B = C) stays the same at all levels. But at the management level, the raw product is no longer newspapers, food, lawns, or tax receipts. A manager's core responsibilities include two primary raw products (what a person is given or placed in charge of), the first of which is the front-line employees themselves.

In other words, it's not the newspapers, eggs, and tax receipts, it's the people who process those things that are the first "raw product" for a manager.

The second core responsibility in the manager's "raw product" column is the *process* used by those employees. It looks like this:

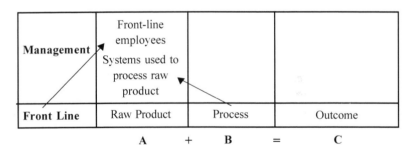

	What someone is given / placed in charge of	What someone does with what they're given	The expected result of working with the raw product through the process
Management	Front-line employees Systems used to process raw product		
Front Line	Raw Product	Process	Outcome
	A	+ B	= C

The possibility of a dual role

It is not uncommon for people serving as lead workers, supervisors, team leaders, and other positions from the management level to also retain responsibilities associated with front-line employees. It's just a fact of life that people wear multiple hats.

If this applies to you, this chapter will give you tremendous insight into what is expected of you when you are wearing a particular hat. The key for success is knowing when to put on your management hat and when to wear your front-line employee hat.

The same will apply to managers who also serve part-time in a leadership capacity.

The manager's outcome

Before getting into what a manager does with his teams and their processes, let's quickly look ahead and note that *efficient operations* are the expected outcome for the manager's level of the Management Matrix. In other words, when all is said and done, most managers are primarily responsible for their team's efficiency. Because a team's efficiency is greatly influenced by how a manager studies and works with the "A" and "B" parts of the formula, it's fair to say that managers set the tone. In essence, they "create the weather" in which their teams must work.

So let's make a weather forecast. What happens if managers ignore the knowledge, skills, and attitudes of their team members? What if, instead of improving their team's capabilities, the managers are grouchy and criticizing, or they center their attention on trivial matters? Using the weather analogy, that behavior is like casting a dark cloud over their teams.

Conversely, if managers are in tune with the capabilities and limitations of their team members, assessing their productivity, and coaching or training them appropriately, it's like providing a fresh breeze and abundant sunshine. And it's those kinds of conditions in which passion is most likely to emerge.

Think back to Gary and Jeff from the previous chapter. Jeff, the Builder, was often seen walking through the production plant, even on the second shift. He'd ask questions and make himself available if someone had a concern. Those behaviors helped Jeff's teams engage their own motivations for creating the best possible product.

However, whenever Gary went through his production plant, chances were good that he'd be focusing only on what was wrong, and someone would get criticized. The weather he created was like a dark cloud that led people to hunker down and ride out the storm.

The manager's "raw products"

Arguments could be made that managers have more things for which they're responsible than people and processes, and I would readily agree. In fact, many are addressed in this book. However, when creating passion-driven teams, a manager has two primary raw products, the first of which is the team members.

In the same way that front-line employees must learn the nuances of their raw product, managers must become familiar with the capabilities, limitations, and nuances of each team member. This basic knowledge enables managers to better delegate, coach, mentor, and train, plus make better decisions in other areas.

Think of how a gourmet chef creates incredibly delicious dishes because of his knowledge of spices and the flavors of different foods. For the chef, a key responsibility is being aware of what flavors are possible by mixing different ingredients. In the same way, it is essential when creating passion-driven teams for managers to be aware of:

➤ What each team member knows.

➤ What skills each team member possesses.

➤ What attitudes are in team members' hearts.

The other main ingredient or "raw product" for managers is the systems their team members use and the processes they follow. Obviously, these will be unique from business to business, but, generally speaking, the systems are whatever procedures or steps front-line employees use to move their raw product along. And just as it's necessary to understand as much as they can about their employees, managers must also understand the systems their team members use.

The Manager's "Processes"

Equipping and training front-line employees is the first part of the manager's *process* responsibilities. At the very least, managers must ensure that team members have the necessary knowledge, skills, and concerns to do their job well. Too many managers skirt around this responsibility, because they've never really learned how to conduct training. It's a sad reality, but it's also a huge mistake. To address this, managers who want passion-driven teams must learn to think like trainers. We'll address training in greater detail in Chapter 12.

The other side of maintaining optimal efficiency is adjusting workflow systems. A team can have highly trained, highly qualified, passion-driven people, but if roadblocks or hiccups exist in their workflow processes, efficiency will be affected.

Whenever obstacles are discovered, managers can use their positional authority to make adjustments or needed changes. Granted, sometimes a company's leader creates environments that make it tough to enact change, but managers let their teams down if they give up without finding a way to make things better.

Adjustments can be as simple as fine-tuning internal team communications or talking with other managers to request changes in how their departments interact. Conversely, managers may need to spend a lot of time gathering data, crunching numbers, and writing proposals for senior management.

As an example of making a simple adjustment, Kathleen managed a team of eight salespeople, but she had a difficult time getting them to complete weekly call reports. These were easy forms to complete. Sales reps merely needed to document who they contacted each day and where they were in the sales process with each prospective client. Not having completed call reports each week led to inefficiencies and lost sales.

To address this issue, Kathleen had the company's webmaster create a call report on the company's Intranet, and created a policy that the sale reps must complete the form each week or their commission vouchers would not be sent to payroll.

Needless to say, the percentage of completed call reports went from 25 to 100 percent, and Kathleen noticed an immediate increase in sales.

In another example, Barbara also needed to make some changes, but her process wasn't quite so easy. As the director of quality control at a fuel storage facility, she saw that her team was spending unnecessary time collecting fuel samples from locations that were difficult to access. A brainstorming session with her team revealed that sample valves could be relocated, and, if they were, each person on the team could save between one and two hours a week.

Unfortunately, such a proposal required plenty of documentation. Barbara collected data from other engineers and estimated the cost of installing the new valves, but she also estimated the cost savings to the company due to the reduced amount of time required to collect samples.

In the end, Barbara submitted a 12-page proposal to senior management, complete with graphs, illustrations, and a clear connection of how the change would improve the company's bottom line. She did a lot of work, but her proposal was accepted.

It may seem simplistic to suggest that people and processes are at the core of a manager's responsibilities. But, unfortunately, too many organizations overlook or neglect teaching their managers the vital nature of these fundamental factors, let alone why they should become experts in them. When managers give little attention to these components, the likelihood of achieving and maintaining a desirable level of efficiency is greatly reduced.

By the way, in the next chapter we'll explore some of the common problems that arise when these core responsibilities are either ignored or given lower priority. The truth is you might be inhibiting your team and not even be aware of it! But, for now, let's finish looking at the manager's level of the matrix.

Assess and Adjust

Similar to how front-line employees must assess their work and make adjustments if necessary, managers must also assess to see if they're achieving their desired level of efficiency. If efficiency is less than optimal, it's the manager's responsibility to analyze, and then do one or both of the following:

➤ Adjust how they're training and placing people.

➤ Alter how they're making adjustments in their team's systems.

In addition, another area for adjustments is in the personnel themselves. Are people in the right positions?

When it comes to repositioning people, I like the analogy used by Jim Collins. In his best-selling book *Good to Great*, Collins points out that not only is it important to get the right people on the bus, it's equally important to have those people sitting in the right seats. Talented team members who are who placed in the wrong positions can diminish a team's efficiency.

To illustrate, let's consider the management team of a West Coast company that was filled with talented people. Unfortunately, at least half of them were in the wrong seats on the bus. The facilities manager was educated in human resources and had the personality for it. The HR manager had both the skills and the personality for quality control. The operations manager had an extensive background in accounting. It was almost as if they had been playing musical chairs. Three or four other people were also working outside their core strengths. Each was doing okay in their roles, but they could have been superstars if they were working in positions more suitable to their expertise.

It's not that these people weren't talented, they were just sitting in the wrong seats, and it showed in more ways than one. This was a clear case of the senior manager (their team leader) not fulfilling a key responsibility. It wasn't until he was replaced that people got moved around to positions that better suited them—with a corresponding improvement in both morale and the company's bottom line.

To re-emphasize a previous point, caution should be the rule when you think about moving people to more appropriate positions. A manager must not only be aware of the knowledge, skills, and attitudes of the people he's moving around, but also calculate the ripple effects of such actions in light of the bigger picture. Blindly reassigning people without such knowledge is often a dangerous exercise because you've not thought through the consequences.

In fact, whenever you make adjustments realize it's not wise to make them in a knee-jerk fashion. You'll want to consider all changes with an organization's mission, vision, and values in mind.

Final Thoughts for Managers

As I mentioned earlier, managers have many other responsibilities, and we'll dig deeply into some of them throughout the book. But at the core of everything sits this vital formula that too many managers are never taught. My strong recommendation is to memorize this matrix. And if you position these managerial responsibilities to be the hub of your mindset, you are strengthening the conditions in which you can create passion-driven teams.

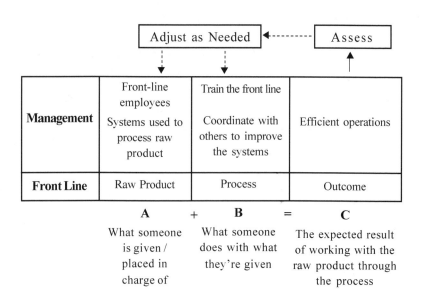

	Adjust as Needed ◄-------- Assess		
Management	Front-line employees Systems used to process raw product	Train the front line Coordinate with others to improve the systems	Efficient operations
Front Line	Raw Product	Process	Outcome
	A	**+ B**	**= C**
	What someone is given / placed in charge of	What someone does with what they're given	The expected result of working with the raw product through the process

The Leadership Level

For leaders, the A + B = C formula remains, but again the factors are different at this level. Here is a list of the leader's *raw product*:

1. The ideas (of where the company could or should be going).
2. The horizon.
3. The realistic capabilities of your organization.

Ideas of where the company could or should be going include the company's vision and mission, but it's also much more than that. Oftentimes leaders have an uncanny instinct or inspiration of how their companies can grow. Many have a gift for sensing opportunities and possibilities. In the Management Matrix, I classify ideas as a raw product. After all, leaders are ultimately in charge of them. It's not that others throughout the organization cannot or should not have ideas, but rather it's the leadership level that's ultimately responsible for collecting and considering them.

The second raw product is what I call the horizon. In geological terms, *horizon* means where the Earth and the sky appear to meet. In astronomy, it is the edge of the universe that is visible. In other words, it is all the light that has reached the Earth thus far; the extent of what we can see.

When applying the term to business, it's looking out at what is likely to happen in the future. The business horizon involves trends, predictions, upcoming legislation, economic forecasts, advances in technology, and much more. The better a leader understands the horizon, the better he is able to follow through on the rest of his responsibilities.

Finally, the third raw product for leadership is the realistic capabilities of the organization. Again, this is something over which leadership is ultimately responsible, so therefore it is a raw product.

To provide a simple but useful analogy, think of being a river guide for a whitewater rafting company. If you're an experienced guide, you know the river can change, sometimes day-to-day. So, whenever you start a trip down the river, even if you have a good idea of what you'd like to do, you keep your eyes on the horizon—the conditions of the river up ahead—and you remain aware of the capabilities of your oarsmen.

Your ideas, the horizon, and the capabilities of your oarsmen are what you have. They're your raw product. What you do with them as a leader is your process.

The leader's "process"

The *process* responsibilities for leaders include:

1. Communicating ideas throughout the organization.
2. Listening carefully to feedback.
3. Adjusting ideas based on feedback, conditions on the horizon, and organizational capabilities.

It's not enough to communicate ideas throughout an organization. Following through on all three of these responsibilities is important. For example, let's go back to being the river guide. As you're floating down the river, you're looking ahead to determine conditions. You notice a large tree branch sticking up, jammed in some rocks. It's a no-brainer—you need to avoid it (a good *idea*), so you point it out to your crew and shout out a command for those on the right side of the raft to start rowing hard (good *communication*).

But there's a problem. Somehow, everyone on the right side of the raft discovers that their oars are broken, probably from the last set of rapids. When they turn around to tell you that, it's not something you want to hear. Your only reply is, "Just make it happen!! Row—row now!"

By not listening to the feedback or making any adjustments, chances are good that your raft is heading for trouble.

In other words, it's not enough to communicate your intentions. In effective organizations, leaders seek and consider feedback.

Granted, some ideas are highly confidential and must remain so, but it's been my observation that too many leaders go overboard on keeping their ideas secret. If you want to create conditions for passion-driven teams to thrive, sensibly sharing your ideas and getting feedback on them is part of the picture.

One leader I know who does a great job of communicating ideas and getting feedback on them is Scott Freeman, president of Johnson Architects in Meridian, Idaho. Freeman has a policy of taking each employee to lunch at least once a quarter. During that lunch Freeman talks about his ideas for what the company could be doing. The conversation is quite informal and his employees have free rein to speak their mind without repercussion.

Interestingly, Freeman, an architect, says that sometimes he doesn't feel like what he's doing is work. That's understandable, because he succeeded in his profession by doing architectural work: pouring over the details of various projects, creating design documents, incorporating detailed specifications, and double checking his designs. But now that he's at a different level in the organization, his responsibilities have changed. The raw product and the processes of a leader are much different from when his company had only three people and everyone did the work of a front-line employee.

The leader's outcome

At the leadership level, the expected outcome is an *effective organization*. In other words, the company is doing what it *should* be doing.

To achieve that outcome, a leader is:

➤ Keeping an eye on the horizon.

➤ Staying in tune with the capabilities of the organization.

➤ Exploring credible ideas.

➤ Communicating those ideas throughout the organization.

➤ Considering feedback and making any needed adjustments.

Assess and adjust

As with the other levels, leaders must assess whether the company is being effective enough, and then make adjustments in his or her products or processes if needed.

It may be that he's not looking at the appropriate factors on the horizon, or maybe he is overestimating the capabilities of the organization. Maybe the ideas he's been considering have an overwhelming number of hidden roadblocks. Or maybe he's not communicating his ideas well, or not getting feedback from the best sources.

Also, because the dynamics within an organization and the conditions acting upon them are ever-changing, adjustments are almost always necessary to keep an organization effective. Therefore, taking time to adequately assess ideas, the horizon, the organization's capabilities, and communication flow is a vital part of a leader's core responsibilities.

When it's all put together, the Management Matrix looks like this:

In the next chapter we'll consider what happens when managers and team leaders work outside their principal roles or disregard their primary responsibilities.

	Adjust as Needed ◄-------- Assess		
Leadership	Ideas The Horizon Organizational capabilities	Communicate ideas / Seek and consider feedback Make adjustments Enable and advance organizational capabilities	Effective organization
Management	Front-line employees Systems used to process raw product	Train the front line Coordinate with others to improve the systems	Efficient operations
Front Line	Raw product	Process	Outcome

A	+	B	=	C
What someone is given / placed in charge of		What someone does with what they're given		The expected result of working with the raw product through the process

Chapter 3

The Cause of Micromanagement

As a relatively new manager, Karl thought he was doing everything expected of him. But when Judy, his boss, pulled him aside one day and told him things weren't working out so well, Karl was floored. He'd always been a top achiever, but now he'd been told his performance was sub-par. "I need you to supervise and train these people," Judy said, "not micromanage them."

"I'm micromanaging? I don't think so!" thought Karl.

When he worked in production, Karl was highly respected among his peers because he had a natural instinct for product quality. Additionally, he'd learned the production process so well, that if quality control discovered a problem, Karl always knew how to fix it.

When Karl was promoted to management, Judy told him his primary responsibility was meeting production numbers. He was also told that senior management expected the end product to be of the same top quality for which Karl was famous. With that in mind, Karl frequently asked his teams for detailed feedback as a way to maintain information flow so he could offer advice and correct any errant tendencies. He was regularly seen on the production line giving detailed instructions at various workstations if things didn't seem right to him. Karl saw this as managing. His team saw it as micromanaging.

Micromanagement Defined

Obviously, Karl wasn't made aware of the Management Matrix and his core responsibilities. As a manager, Karl should have been training and equipping his employees while keeping an eye on the various systems for ways to improve them. He certainly had the knowhow. He just didn't have the right approach for going about it.

If you think of a micromanager as someone who dictates every action and every decision for everyone on the team, you're pretty much on target. Our friends at *Webster's Dictionary* define micromanagement as: "to manage with great or excessive control or attention to details."

The symptoms

Micromanagement can be diagnosed when some or all of the following is observed in managers:

➤ They appear frustrated that nobody is "getting it" or taking things as seriously as they do.

➤ They want frequent status updates, even when things are operating normally.

➤ They are quick to point out errors and mistakes of team members.

➤ They have an overloaded task list, but their teams are looking for things to do.

➤ They get upset if they're not consulted before decisions are made.

➤ They'll take back delegated tasks to do them quicker or better themselves.

Additionally, micromanagement may be a correct diagnosis when some or all of the following is observed on a team:

➤ A team experiences high turnover.

➤ Team members feel nothing they do is ever good enough.

➤ Team members are required to "check with the boss" before making any decision.

➤ Team members no longer take initiative.

➤ Team members are responsible for results, but have little or no input for how to achieve them.

The Cause

The stage is often set for micromanagement to emerge when companies promote a front-line employee into management simply because he or she is a top performer. Companies regularly make erroneous assumptions in thinking that a person who does a good job as a front-line employee will excel in the role of manager. They fail to realize that these are totally different roles with totally different responsibilities.

Compounding the problem is a new manager's psychological need for success. After all, front-line employees who get promoted are often internally driven to excel. But when people aren't taught how to succeed in their new managerial role, it's only logical that they'll depend on tried-and-true methods for success that worked for them in the past.

This begs the question: "How do front-line employees know they're being successful?" More often than not they listen for two key words: "Good job."

To illustrate, let's go back to the Management Matrix and put ourselves in the role of a front-line employee. In this role, we're responsible for taking raw product and moving it through a process to achieve a specific outcome. We learn the nuances, capabilities, and limitations of the raw product as well as the systems. And we know we were doing well if we heard those magic words: *good job.*

But hearing "good job" is more than just an ego stroke—it's tied to some very deep motivations. Some people do well so they can get a raise. Others want the satisfaction of knowing they contributed to something bigger than themselves. Some want to be recognized as creative, while others want to know that their work is exactly within standards. Some do well because they want to be promoted, and others do well simply because they wish to be seen as an expert.

Any of these reasons (and more) can be a driving force for us to excel, but the ticket that gets us what we want usually consists of hearing those two magic words: *good job.* Here are some examples:

> ➤ If we want a raise, we learn what we can and work hard to hear "good job" because we believe that if we hear those words often enough, it can translate to a raise.

> ➤ If we're doing creative work and want to be recognized as creative, "good job" tells us we're succeeding in our goal.

> ➤ If we want to get promoted, we study our raw product and processes so we can make the best finished product, because hearing "good job" increases the likelihood of us getting that promotion.

For many, the phrase "good job" is like a currency. Hearing it a lot lets us know we're on the right track for getting what we really want—the raise, the recognition, the promotion, and so on.

Now let's put ourselves in the role of a front-line employee who has just received a promotion. Our drive to succeed has not diminished, plus we want whoever promoted us to believe they made a good choice. In other words, we still want to hear "good job." However, if we are unaware of our new core responsibilities (train our teams and adjust systems) or unclear on how to perform them, it's not uncommon to jump in and fix a problem when one appears on the production line. After all, somebody valued the fact that we mastered the raw product and the processes as a front-line employee, or we wouldn't have been promoted. Besides, when we step in to solve a production problem we'll be putting our proven skills to work. Doing that not only provides a sense of personal satisfaction, it's what we did in the past to hear the words "good job."

If new managers don't receive instruction or mentoring for how to function properly in a managerial role, they often turn to behaviors that previously earned them a sense of approval.

Like we've pointed out, stepping in to fix a production problem is a common way to fulfill the very real human drive to be valued and feel successful.

Such are the most common seeds of micromanagement.

More cause: Under-treating the problem

Another cause for the emergence of micromanagement is management training that is well-intended, but does not accomplish its goals.

It's similar to a growing problem in healthcare today where some doctors are under-treating medical conditions. The unfortunate result is unnecessary pain for the patient. In the same way, undertraining a new manager often results in unnecessary pain for the manager—and his team.

To their credit, numerous companies provide training for new managers. Unfortunately, many of these efforts provide inadequate results. The reason? Most new manager classes provide basic knowledge and understanding about management responsibilities, but students receive very little practice in actually applying what's taught. Think of it as attending a class on how to ride a bicycle when you've never ridden one before. You could pass tests proving you know the names of the bicycle's parts and even explaining the theory of how a bicycle works, but if they never let you get on a bike and actually ride it, your mental ability to recall data probably won't help you with necessary physical skills such as hand-eye coordination and balance.

Similarly, one manager compared most of the management training he received to an astronomy class he had in college. He studied his textbooks and passed the exams, but never once did he look through a telescope or physically locate any stars. When he finished the class he could explain the theories and he knew the terminology, but he didn't know how to put his new knowledge into practice with the actual handling of a telescope.

Sadly, the core responsibilities of managers (training people and adjusting systems) are even missing from many business degree programs. Jake is a middle manager with a Bachelor of Arts in management. He tells me that his degree program did not equip him to think like a manager. "I learned the buzzwords, the accounting programs, and all about 'management,' but I never learned how to manage a group of people. Nobody ever taught us how to operate as a team, to make adjustments based on feedback and what we were seeing."

Essentially, the heart of the problem is that new managers have a difficult time shifting their thinking out of their area of specialty and into their management and team leader responsibilities. Even if they're lucky enough to get management training, rarely do they get a chance to practice what they've learned.

Even more cause: fear

So far we've acknowledged that micromanagement emerges out of a drive for a sense of approval (hearing "good job") and having the problem undertreated by those who "ought" to know better.

However, a third factor can also cause micromanagement to emerge, and we shouldn't ignore it. The third source is *fear*. Some people choose micromanagement behaviors because they are afraid of the consequences of failing. Whereas hearing "good job" is a positive motivator, fear is negative motivator—and, some would argue, more powerful. For example,

➤ People fear that work will not be done right, so they do it themselves.

➤ People fear losing credit for a job well done, so they make sure they have their hands in the actual "end product."

➤ People fear their influence will wane if other front-line employees step up and become production superstars.

➤ People fear being labeled as a do-nothing. An uninformed but common mindset adopted in some blue-collar circles is that unless you're getting your hands dirty, you're not working.

➤ Fear often freezes people, but in the case of micromanagement, fear can drive people to action.

People want to succeed, especially after they've been promoted. But if people are not made aware of their new core responsibilities, if they're not trained nor mentored well, or if they allow fear to influence their choices, it's quite possible for micromanagement behaviors to emerge.

Because it's nearly impossible to create a passion-driven team in an atmosphere of micromanagement, we'll take the next chapter and look at ways to cure this common workplace problem.

Summary

> Micromanagement is defined as "to manage with great or excessive control or attention to details."

> Signs can be observed in managers and in teams that micromanagement is occurring.

> Some people choose to micromanage because doing so may result in hearing "good job."

> Some people micromanage because their management training was insufficient or ineffective.

> Some people micromanage because they fear certain consequences if they don't.

Chapter 4

The Cure for Micromanagement

To cure micromanagement, organizations must actively teach that each level in the Management Matrix requires:

➤ a different level of thinking/a change in how people think.

➤ a different set of core competencies/responsibilities/duties.

➤ an ability to assess and adjust based on feedback.

Furthermore, each position in the company requires:

➤ a clearly defined list of competencies/responsibilities/duties.

➤ an ongoing training and mentoring schedule.

Managers and team leaders must commit to understanding and applying themselves to the core responsibilities for the management role. As a reminder, here is the management level of the Management Matrix:

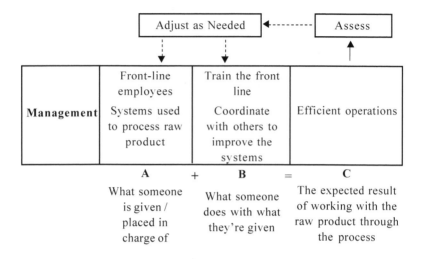

The above requirements are the primary prescription. Obviously more can be done, but these are the essentials for what an organization can do to prevent and cure micromanagement. (Note: If you realize you've been micromanaging or have been accused of it by others, and your organization doesn't have these factors in place, see the section titled "Curing Micromanagement on Your Own" later in this chapter.)

To really understand the cure, let's take a closer look at each part of the primary prescription. In the first part, companies must teach that each level in the Management Matrix requires a change in how people think.

A different level of thinking is required

Looking back at Karl's situation in the previous chapter, it's clear he would have benefited from learning to think at a new level. He was with his company for years, building an excellent reputation as a craftsman. Everyone recognized that he produced the best his company had to offer, but after he was promoted his former peers complained about being micromanaged. Instead of educating people in what to do, Karl either kept a tight leash on everybody or simply did the work himself. He didn't know he needed to focus on and think about a new set of responsibilities.

Judy, his boss, had made the common mistake of assuming that because Karl was gifted at handling his front-line responsibilities, he would quickly convert into being an effective manager. Because of that assumption, she didn't give Karl a plan for transitioning into his new position. She failed to make sure he knew that being at a new level in the organization required a new level of thinking.

A different set of core competencies required

If the first part of the prescription is knowing that each level in an organization requires a different level of thinking, the secont part is knowing that each position requires a well-defined list of responsiblities. For managers, that means a fairly detailed framework for what's expected and guidance on how to get there. Just giving someone a title without a job descprition, clear-cut expectations, and feedback sets the person up to fail.

Judy gave Karl a cursory overview of his new duties, but nothing in terms of mentoring or training to ensure he was equipped for his new responsibilities. That's also what happened to Art when he was seen as the most competoent person on his team and subsequently promoted to manager.

His boss called him in, told him he was getting a title and a team to oversee, and asked Art to prepare a job description for himself. Art developed numerous drafts, but each one was rejected. After each rejection, Art asked for feedback. Although there was a lot of talk, clarification was always elusive. This led to tension between the two of them, and before long. Art set aside the majority of his managerial responsibilities. Not only did expectations of him remain unclear, but Art wanted the satisfaction of getting things done. He returned to doing what he knew best and focused his efforts on the core work of the department.

After six months, Art's boss decided Art was a micromanager. Without receiving any coaching or guidance, Art was told he was "not a good fit," and was terminated.

This all-too-common tragedy plays itself out in organizations every day. Whether someone is promoted from within or hired as a manager, organizations shoot themselves in the foot if they believe that skilled and experienced employees don't need a road map and some guidance when shifting to a new role.

Assess and adjust based on feedback

To continue the prescription, companies must also make sure people "assess and adjust." We can think of this as a desire for self-correction based on trustworthy input. There are many ways to do this, and we'll examine some of them later in this chapter, but if companies don't enable people to receive and act on feedback, micromanagement is likely to occur.

Specific Nuts and Bolts

The primary prescription emphasizes three beliefs an organization should teach and what groundwork should be in place to minimize micromanagement. Now let's look closer at the nuts and bolts involved in actually placing someone in a management or team leader role:

> ➤ Begin with the end in mind: Clearly explain what knowledge, skills, and attitudes are expected in the new position.

> ➤ Assess each new manager's capabilities and compare them to the list of responsibilities for the position.

> ➤ Institute training/mentoring/coaching to address any gaps, so managers can reach the established level of expectation.

> ➤ Give the new manager regular feedback, reinforcing all professional growth and development.

Clearly explain what knowledge, skills, and attitudes are expected in the new position

First things first, each position needs a well-written job description. I'm not talking about a generic, ancient document that's locked away in an HR drawer. This must be a current list of duties and tasks.

If you don't have clear, detailed job descriptions, I recommend using a "Table Top Job Analysis" method, as it makes fairly short work of the process. An overview of the practice looks like this:

1. Form a small group of experts for the job in question. People who already do the job well are best. If the position is brand new, select people who understand what will be expected of the person doing the job. Ideally, your group should be three to seven people.

2. Have each person in the group make a list of duties required of someone doing that job. For clarification, a *duty* is a general area of responsibility, whereas a *task* is a specific action that, when combined with other tasks, fulfills a duty. Here's an example taken from a Safety Director's job description. Notice that

the duty and each task begin with what the person must do. A general guideline is to have no less than five and no more than 14 duties for any one job.

Duty:

Oversee emergency response teams.

Tasks:

◆ Identify deficiencies in the emergency plan.

◆ Develop emergency response skills in office personnel.

◆ Create response teams and appoint leaders.

◆ Educate all personnel on potential emergencies.

◆ Schedule and conduct emergency response training.

◆ Evaluate emergency team effectiveness.

3. After each person has a list of duties, have someone read out loud one duty from his or her list. Others in the group will likely have that duty listed, or something similar to it. As a group, decide if it is a duty or a task that supports a larger duty. If it is a duty, come to a consensus on the best wording and write it down.

4. For the second duty, have the next person read a duty from his or her list (going around the room keeps things fair and fresh). Repeat this process until everyone's duty list has been addressed.

5. Have the group prioritize the final duty list for what is most important. It is strongly recommended to keep the Management Matrix core responsibilities at or near the top.

After creating a master duty list, take each duty one-by-one and use this same method to identify the tasks required for each duty. Here's an example of how a finished duty/task list might be formatted:

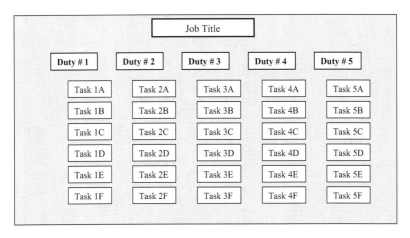

The result of this effort gives you a phenomenally powerful tool for hiring, training, managing, and measuring performance. (For more-detailed instructions on how to conduct a Table Top Job Analysis, visit *www.passiondriventeams.com*.)

Other things to consider

Along with a duty and task list, job descriptions can also list what knowledge, skills, and attitudes are required for success in a position. This can include specific analytical or evaluative abilities, required physical capabilities, and specific things about which a person should be concerned.

The main thing to remember in all of this is that you're creating a list of expectations for a particular position. Granted, tasks may crop up that seem nebulous, but people will deal with those as they come. Just don't keep this in a file drawer! One great benefit of having an up-to-date duty and task list is that it also serves as a checklist for what to measure when assessing a manager's capabilities.

Whether promoting a new manager from within or hiring someone into a position, use your job description as a springboard for dialogue to discover what pertinent knowledge, skills, and attitudes a person is bringing to the table.

Assess each new manager's capabilities and compare them to the list of responsibilities

You can use a wide variety of assessment tools to compare what behaviors and attitudes a person naturally has to the behaviors and attitudes that will be most appropriate for a specific job. The important thing is to first benchmark the job.

Use assessment tools that pinpoint specific talents necessary for successful job performance. Complementary assessments can then help you determine the talents and tendencies of someone either working in or being considered for that position. If differences are discovered, it doesn't mean the person is unqualified, it simply means a bit of adapting may be necessary. The assessment process helps you identify what adjustments might be needed.

Using assessment tools was helpful for Brandi, a regional manager who was frustrated with the performance of Karen, a rising star in the company. Karen was overseeing a product development team, but after nine months of floundering and "majoring in the minors," Karen's team was frustrated, and so was Brandi. The two women decided to use personality assessment tools to discover where things weren't connecting.

They asked a management coach to go over the assessment results with each person; first individually, and then with the two of them together. In less than a few hours, they uncovered vast differences in their basic communication preferences.

Both acknowledged that neither style was better than the other—they were just different. Additionally, it became clear that Karen was inadvertently sending mixed messages to her team. "It's like I was speaking German and my team was speaking Swahili," Karen said of the experience. "But once I saw how I was being misunderstood, I knew how to make adjustments in how I did things."

This part of the micromanagement cure—assessing capabilities and comparing them to job requirements—is often overlooked because it doesn't carry a sense of urgency. But, without it, it's akin to seeing your doctor for a serious pain and he writes a prescription without asking any questions or doing any tests. You certainly wouldn't want your doctor scheduling you for surgery if all you needed was a muscle relaxer, and you wouldn't want him giving you a muscle relaxer if what you really needed was surgery. Properly assessing a problem is the first step in curing it.

Give special attention to this step. A wide variety of assessment tools are on the market, and they provide tremendous insights. For a detailed list of some of the tools you can use and how to use them, visit *www.passiondriventeams.com.*

Institute training/mentoring/coaching to address any gaps

After differences between actual proficiencies and job requirements are identified, it's time to create a plan for how to bridge the gaps. For optimal buy-in, this plan should be created as a cooperative effort between the new manager and his supervisor, and the plan should address as much of the big picture as possible.

Central to most training and mentoring plans are technical, managerial, and interpersonal skills. More detailed aspects can include:

Contract management	Project management
Accounting	Marketing
Communication skills	Conflict resolution
Training/facilitation skills	Mentoring skills
Problem-solving	Delegating

Obviously, whatever training/mentoring/coaching plan you create should be based on what's needed for success in a specific job. Each position is unique in its own way, so training requirements must be adjusted accordingly for different positions.

Additionally, don't expect overnight change. Becoming a fully transitioned manager can take years. Too many organizations mistakenly believe that a new manager should be up to speed in just a few months, but research clearly shows this is false.

A study tracked the progress of 2,600 new managers during a five-year span, only 25 percent were considered to have successfully transitioned into their new role at the conclusion of the study. It's hard to argue with the facts, and that's a horrible track record. It's also a screaming indictment of how badly companies are failing in equipping their managers to be successful.

Unfortunately, the problem may actually be getting worse. The Emerge Leadership Research Institute collected data showing that between 2005 and 2008 the percentage of fully transitioned managers declined from 25 percent to just 16 percent.

Jim Wentworth, president of the Emerge Leadership Group, says that companies simply aren't taking the time to ensure successful transitions. "They want new managers to meet company goals, and they don't care how the goals are met. As a result, managers are giving minimal attention to managerial responsibilities and doing much of the work themselves."

Wentworth says that it's not uncommon for managers to spend up to 85 percent of their day doing work that would normally be assigned to front-line employees.

Plainly, new managers are going to do whatever it takes to meet expectations. If company expectations do not include learning the core responsibilities for the management level, new managers ignore them and slip into micromanagement.

With this in mind, training/mentoring/coaching plans become vital, and new managers must become ravenous students of their new responsibilities. This cannot be emphasized enough. Becoming a new manager is like starting out in an entirely new job, and a shift in thinking is required. Seeing a bigger picture is a necessity, and many new skills are essential for success.

It's essential to realize that none of this happens by osmosis. The following statement may be considered exaggerated, but it drives home a key truth:

The only skill that made you successful as a frontline employee that will also make you successful as a manager is the ability to learn.

Just because people are competent in their front-line role doesn't mean they won't need help learning how to be a good manager. It's an entirely new job. People must learn new responsibilities, and companies must train, coach, and mentor people to be successful in them. Without such learning, micromanagement is almost guaranteed to be (or remain) a problem.

Give the new manager regular feedback, reinforcing all professional growth and development

Remember "good job"? New managers still want to know if they're doing what's expected. This is why coaching and mentoring are so vital in the training process. Routine conversations—sometimes on a daily basis, especially in the beginning—with a seasoned manager are vital for new managers to keep things straight. Such conversations should contain suggestions for improvement, as well as specific examples of what's been going well. Too much of one without the other can have negative consequences:

➤ Coaching/mentoring sessions with only
   suggestions for improvement leave a new
   manager demoralized, wondering if he's doing
   anything right at all.

➤ Sessions with only praise for what's going well
   can become meaningless.

This doesn't mean the two areas of focus need equal time, just that both are valuable, and each serves a need.

Why are feedback conversations vital? Without them, it's easy for new managers to slip into micromanagement. Consider what happened to Karen. She had a long history of success in her tech position at an aerospace technology firm. Shortly after her promotion to supervisor, she attended a highly regarded two-week management training class. Just as in her technical position, she excelled in the training class and received high marks from the instructor.

Unfortunately, not long after returning to work Karen began criticizing and nitpicking her staff for minor issues. She was unable to separate real issues from trivial matters. She wrote people up for small infractions, she acted indifferently when employees brought up concerns, and didn't spend much time in training, planning, or organizing. Much of her days were spent going over each team member's work with a fine-tooth comb, and then sending projects back for correction.

Within seven months, five people from her team had requested transfers, and two simply found work elsewhere and quit. The staff that remained had lost all respect for her. Although complaints had been filed, neither HR nor Karen's immediate supervisor did any counseling, coaching, or mentoring with her. After a year, senior management decided Karen wasn't cutting it and fired her.

This tragedy, not unlike Art's, might have been prevented if Karen had received mentoring and coaching after her two weeks of training. Think of the turmoil that the employees (and their families) endured simply because Karen wasn't being mentored. The ripple-effects of unbridled micromanagement are far-reaching—and expensive.

When assigning someone to serve in a mentoring role, choose carefully. Mentors should be trained in how to perform that function. Here are some good do's and don'ts for mentoring and coaching:

: Don't force new managers to adopt practices that aren't comfortable for them.

Do find out what's comfortable for them, and help them find ways to make it work.

: Don't suggest they do things that run counter to their values. Value systems are tied to a person's sense of right and wrong.

Do help new managers understand how their value system helps the company meet its objectives.

: Don't do all the talking.

Do ask a lot of questions that lead people to think. Good coaching and mentoring doesn't mean having all the answers; it means asking good questions. Yes, advice and suggestions can be helpful, but they shouldn't be everything.

❢ Don't act like a know-it-all.

Do bite your tongue and ask questions. See the previous point.

❢ Don't criticize every mistake.

Minor mistakes can be yellow flags, but they certainly shouldn't take over a conversation. If you think your protégé manager made a mistake, questions such as "What were your other options?" and "What did you learn from that?" will get a new manager thinking—not wincing from a verbal rebuke.

❢ Don't encourage your new manager to be dependent on you.

Do offer praise and recognition to reinforce independent decisions that show initiative and good decision-making.

❢ Don't take responsibility for a new manager's projects.

Your protégé's workload is not your direct responsibility. As much as you might be tempted to step in and help out, it's often better to teach them how to manage their projects better.

❢ Don't vent any of your own frustrations to the new manager.

If you have gripes about anyone or anything, your time spent mentoring should be focused on the manager and his issues, not yours. The topic of conversation should always revolve around the manager!

❢ Don't allow the manager to become dependent on you.

Do encourage the manager to think by asking questions such as "What's your take on it?" "What do you think is the best course of action?" "What leads to you that conclusion?" "What are some of the possible ripple effects?" Obviously, advice can and should be given.

The sensible thing to do is wait until a situation would benefit from your input, and then ask if the manager would like your thoughts on a matter.

❢ Don't be too busy to meet.

Although you shouldn't let a manager become dependent on you, it's similarly unwise to be unavailable. The trick is finding a balance of "being there" and asking good questions that help a person think. If at all possible, have a purpose for each meeting. Planning for dialogue around a specific topic helps the new manager place value on your meetings.

Certainly a lot more could be discussed, but this is a good start. It's fair to say that whoever is assigned a mentor's role should know how to be a mentor!

Curing Micromanagement on Your Own

If you've come to realize you're micromanaging, or you've been accused of it by others and your organization doesn't have the mechanisms in place to help, rest assured there's hope. It will require more focus and effort on your part, but it's certainly feasible.

Using the material in this chapter as your guide, your first task will be to change your thinking. Review the Management Matrix outlined in Chapter 2. Understand that your primary responsibilities are to train your team members and monitor the efficiency of the systems they're using, making any adjustments as necessary. Here is a mantra that might help:

> **Each level in the organization requires a different level of thinking.**

Memorize that phrase. Then visualize yourself letting go of the thinking that made you successful as a front-line employee and mentally see yourself picking up a new type of thinking—a type of thinking that positions you as a coordinator and trainer. Also, think of yourself as starting off in a whole new job (because you are!).

Yes, the people who promoted you may push for you to meet certain numbers, but you will be much better off when you can make sure everyone on your team has been trained in what you know. Sometimes this means you'll need to "paint the train while it's moving," and squeeze training tidbits in wherever you can. But, by all means, train your teams in the nuances of their raw product, the processes they must use, and how to solve problems (see Chapter 12 for help in how to be a good trainer).

Whatever you do, don't fall into the misguided thinking that if you teach everyone what you know, there will be no need for you. This mindset is common, but it's a fallacy. When senior management sees you can train others to do what you do, your value to the company increases because you can duplicate yourself.

Also, when you train others to troubleshoot and fix problems in addition to performing well, you can spend more of your time performing higher-level managerial tasks. If nothing else, you'll have more time for planning ahead, which is great because good planning minimizes crisis and "fires." Senior managers like teams to run smoothly without a lot of fires to put out, because then they don't have to worry about them!

Don't think you have time to train your people? Here's another mantra for you:

Slower up front equals faster down the road.

Memorize that phrase, too. Yes, it may take a bit more time to get people trained than if you simply jumped in and fixed problems yourself. But which option gives you more time in the long run: giving someone a fish every day, or teaching that person how to fish on their own?

Remember Jeff, the senior production manager from Chapter 1? He listened very carefully to what his teams were telling him and he asked people for their input. More often than not, they had good ideas for how to fix problems, it's just that they wanted someone with experience to tell them it was a good choice. That's what Jeff did. Sure, he could have told people what to do to fix problems; that would have been fast and easy. It even might have made him feel important. But he knew that if his teams were to become passionate about their work they'd have to invest something of themselves into it.

Yes, it was time-consuming to let people think through problems and articulate solutions. And, if they weren't quite getting it, Jeff had to think of ways to lead them toward the solution without spelling it out for them. That approach took longer, and often felt like extra work, but Jeff was a believer in "slower up front equals faster down the road." He knew that by taking 10 extra minutes now he'd be saving countless hours in the weeks, months, and years to come.

Clarify Your Role and Responsibilities

Art had a tough time getting clarity on his job description, and you may encounter similar difficulties. But here's the difference: Art eventually gave up—you don't have to. Be persistant. Keep asking for clarification and help with formulating your job description as you go. Obviously you'll need to be careful not to ruffle people's feathers, but persistence has much value. Keep in mind these conversations don't have to be confrontational. Informal dialogue will be just as effective as long as you keep building your list of responsibilities.

To really hone in on learning what's needed to break out of micromanagement, take each responsibility assigned to you and outline the knowledge and skills needed for you to excel. Chapter 12 will help you create specific learning objectives so you know you're getting it.

Conduct a Self-Analysis

Again, this can be tough if you're doing it on your own, but you'll be amazed at how many people are willing to help (both up and down the chain of command) if you go to them with something like this:

> **"I'm aware that I've been guilty of micromanaging, and I'm trying to break out of it. What are some things you think I can do—or not do—to be a better manager?"**

It's a gutsy move, because what you hear may cut like a knife. It will certainly be humbling, and you may need to fight like crazy to keep from being defensive. But if you remain objective, take notes, commit to repairing relationships, and work on what you hear, you will have a firsthand assessment telling you exactly what's needed for you to improve.

If the situation calls for it, you may even want to apologize for any behaviors or attitudes that have offended people, and tell them you're committed to addressing those issues to become a better manager. This doesn't mean grovel. It just means show yourself as honestly committed to improving. It's a fair bet that the people you approach in this effort will be quite supportive.

Get yourself a coach

If your organization doesn't incorporate mentoring or coaching into its management philosophy, look outside the company and find yourself a coach. But don't hire just anyone who calls himself a coach. Find someone with a track record of success helping people in your line of work. Check his or her credentials, and check his or her references. And most of all, make sure you feel comfortable working with whomever you choose.

Also, don't just choose the least expensive option. Expect to pay consultant's rates, even if you have to squeeze it out of your own pocket. If you'll recall, this is what Cynthia did (in Chapter 1), and it paid off for her in the form of several promotions. Once you find someone to work with, keep the following in mind:

1. Be clear about the purpose of the coaching relationship. Mutually come to an agreement on what knowledge, skills, and attitudes you wish to acquire, and how success will be measured.

2. Be clear about the ground rules. You should have the right to ask for advice, as well as reject any advice offered. You're trying to get help for you to be a better you—not become a carbon copy of your coach. A coach should be a partner with you on your path of professional growth.

3. Be clear about how the coaching relationship will end. Coaching relationships are rarely long-term agreements. Commitments in three- or six-month time chunks are reasonable, but either party should have the right to say "done" if it's felt that the relationship is not meeting expectations.

Find more about coaching relationships at *www.passiondriventeams.com.*

Coaching should be part of your equation, because regular follow- up, accountability, and feedback are essential ingredients for lasting change. As human beings we are creatures of habit, and changing our habits requires more than sheer willpower (Chapter 6 addresses this from your perspective as a team leader). It was true what my own coach told me: "You can't change yourself." So the bottom line is, if you're trying to cure micromanagement within yourself, make sure you find a good management coach.

Summary

Micromanagement Causes:

➤ Micromanagement is often born out of a person's desire to fulfill an internal motivation.

➤ People who are driven to succeed usually want to know they're being successful.

➤ The "currency" connecting success with internal motivation is often the phrase "good job."

➤ A lot of management training undertreats the problem by providing little (if any) practice.

Organizational Necessities:

➤ Each level in an organization requires its own level of thinking.

➤ Each position must have clearly defined responsibilities.

➤ Ongoing training and mentoring is needed throughout an organization.

New managers must receive:

➤ A clear explanation of responsibilities.

➤ An assessment revealing the gaps between "what is" and "what's needed."

➤ Training, coaching, and mentoring.

➤ Regular feedback.

Chapter 5

Becoming an Expert About the People You Manage

Perhaps you've heard of Emotional Intelligence. If you haven't, here are two reasons why you should know what it is:

1. Studies show that top performers are more likely than average performers to have high Emotional Intelligence.
2. Emotional Intelligence is learnable.

Psychologists differ on how to define this growing area of study, but one thing is certain: Research conducted throughout the past few decades has resulted in a growing mountain of evidence showing higher levels of Emotional Intelligence in people who are considered successful, with lower levels in people considered to be average and below average performers.

Emotional Intelligence (sometimes referred to as an *Emotional Intelligence Quotient* or "EQ"), is commonly defined as: The ability, capacity, or skill to perceive, assess, and manage the emotions of one's self, of others, and of groups.

That's a good start, because understanding the influence of emotions in the workplace is vital. But becoming an expert about the people on your teams means learning about more than perceiving, assessing, and managing emotions. Other aspects to look at include:

> different ways people think.

> behavioral tendencies.

> individual motivations.

When we take these factors into account and consider what we're supposed to do with Emotional Intelligence, we can offer the following, alternative definition of EQ:

An ability to perceive and assess one's own and other people's emotions, tendencies, and desires, and then choose the best course of action based on those perceptions to obtain the best result.

Gaining Emotional Intelligence is valuable for mastering one of the core responsibilities of managers and team leaders as outlined in the Management Matrix: Becoming aware of the capabilities, limitations, and nuances of the people on our teams. Therefore, it makes total sense for managers and team leaders to become students of EQ.

If you're looking for more evidence to show why this endeavor is worth your time, Cary Cherniss, PhD, of the Consortium for Research on Emotional Intelligence in Organizations, has a great article you can find with a quick online search entitled "The Business Case for Emotional Intelligence," which you can find with a quick online search. In that article, Cherniss quotes numerous studies showing how higher levels of EQ result in more productivity and profitability. I'm not talking 5 and 10 percent differences, I'm talking increases in productivity and profitability of more than 100 percent. That difference is just too big to ignore. Even if you achieved half that increase by improving your EQ, it would be worth every ounce of your effort.

But where's the best place to start? Understanding people can take a lifetime. Additionally, we can't afford to guess about people and be wrong.

Using Assessments

The absolute quickest way to understanding the different ways people think, their behavioral tendencies, and their individual motivators is by using assessments. As we pointed out in the previous chapter, if you went to your doctor because of an ailment, you'd want him running lab tests to find out what's really going on before making any critical decisions on your treatment. Why should it be any different for managers who must decide what actions are needed to build effective, productive, passion-driven teams?

Just as with doctors, one bad decision by a manager can cause significant pain for employees as well as the organization. Therefore, knowing which "tests" to order is important for managers to accurately assess the thinking styles, behavioral tendencies, and motivations of the people on their teams.

Numerous assessment tools are available on the market, and each one focuses on a particular aspect of personality. However, space is not available in this book to describe the pros and cons of each one. The Website *www.passiondriventeams.com* provides an extensive list detailing the uses of many assessment tools along with links for how to obtain them or get additional information.

Even so, we will take a brief look at three of the more common assessment tools. These tools provide tremendous insight into the different ways people think, their behavioral tendencies, and their individual motivators, plus they are very easy to use. To expedite your journey on becoming an expert about the people you manage, these assessments are strongly recommended:

Area Being Assessed:	Type of Assessment to Use:
Different ways people think	Myers-Briggs Type Indicator
Behavioral tendencies	DISC assessments
Individual motivators	Workplace Motivators

Different Ways People Think

The most popular assessment for measuring different ways people think is the *Myers-Briggs Type Indicator*, commonly referred to as the MBTI. Millions of people take this assessment each year, as it does a great job of identifying a person's preferences in four spectrums, or scales. You should familiarize yourself with what each of these spectrums measure, as it will help you understand the tendencies, preferences, strengths, and weaknesses of yourself (yes, you should complete one of these, too), as well as those on your teams.

The MBTI measures people's preferences in the following four areas:

1. **Where do people send their energy and how do they get energized?**

   They may direct their energy outward and get recharged by being with others, or they may focus inward and get recharged by being alone.

2. **How do people perceive information?**

   They may first notice the "here and now," or they may intuitively see implications for the future.

3. **How do people process information on the way to a decision?**

   They may process information objectively and without emotion, or they may do so with plenty of expression and a display of feelings.

4. How do they make and implement decisions?

They may decide quickly and stick closely to schedules, or they may stay flexible and spontaneous.

Again, we recommend the MBTI to find out the different ways people think.

A note of caution: Always look at these assessments as inherently neutral. Do not ascribe "good" or "bad" to someone's preference. People are just different!

Different Ways People Behave

The most popular tool for measuring how people conduct themselves in various situations is the *DISC assessment*. Just as with the MBTI, millions of people complete DISC assessments each year because they provide excellent insights into a person's behavioral tendencies.

DISC assessments measure people's preferences in the following four areas:

1. How do people behave in the face of problems and challenges?

They may prefer taking charge and solving problems quickly, or they may step back and hope that problems work out if given time.

2. How do people influence other people?

They may be enthusiastic, optimistic, and eager to talk with anybody, or, they may prefer being reserved, skeptical, and somewhat reclusive.

3. How do people behave in terms of workday pace and consistency?

They may prefer a steady, predictable, well-prioritized workday, or, they may enjoy multitasking in a dynamic, changing environment.

4. How do people respond to rules, procedures, and constraints?

They may like analyzing facts and adhering to established protocols, or, they may be boldly independent, following unconventional ideas.

The cool thing about the DISC assessment is it measures observable behavior. And, by learning to ask yourself two key questions about someone, you can identify a person's "core" behavioral style, which gives you great insights as to the best way to talk with that person! (Study DISC communication styles at *www.passiondriventeams.com.*)

Different Internal Motivators

One of the best assessments for measuring the *why* behind someone's behavior is the *Workplace Motivators* assessment. Based on the work of the late psychologist Eduard Spranger, and produced by Target Training International, this tool provides a relative ranking of six primary motivations.

The Workplace Motivator assessment measures people's interests, or motivations, in six areas:

1. How much do people value gaining knowledge/learning new things?

Driven toward learning for its own sake, going beyond the required knowledge base

2. How much do people value financial security?

Driven toward practical endeavors that bring a return on investment

3. How much do people value form, harmony, grace, and symmetry?

Driven toward interpreting life as an artistic progression of events

4. **How much do people value sympathetic, selfless acts to help others?**

   Driven toward humanitarian efforts and community well-being

5. **How much do people value personal power and influence?**

   Driven toward advancement with the ability to direct and control

6. **How much do people value having defined rules and principles for living?**

   Driven toward living according to traditional, orderly systems

Again, these three assessments provide insights into people's thinking styles, their behavioral preferences, and their internal motivators. By using assessments such as these, you gain rapid insight into peoples' strengths and weaknesses. In other words, if you've been hoping for a shortcut in this process of creating passion-driven teams, this is the only one I can recommend because it won't shortchange the process.

Think of assessments as valuable tools for maximizing teamwork and productivity. With the knowledge you gain from assessment results, you are much better equipped to coach, counsel, and develop your team to levels of enduring excellence.

Richard Nelson, the HR manager for Idahoan Foods, LLC, is a strong believer in using assessments for teambuilding. "I see a person's scores on the different assessments and immediately know how he or she is going to work with the rest of the team," he says. "There are strengths and weaknesses associated with each person's scores, but as long as I know what those are, I know what's necessary to bring out the best in those people."

A springboard for conversation

Assessments give you quick insights about people, but don't just throw those insights into a drawer. Sit down with your team members one-on-one and review their results with them. Use the reports generated from each assessment as a springboard for conversation, but be careful. Quite often people are not sure what these assessments are going to tell them. It's not uncommon for people to fear being criticized or even verbally attacked. Therefore, remember that you must create what I call a "safe" environment when working with these assessment tools.

Things to talk about include:

➤ With which findings do they agree? Disagree?

➤ What would they like to see different in themselves?

➤ Which strengths contribute most to the team?

➤ Which weaknesses need the most attention?

➤ Are they aware of how they come across to other people?

You can also use the reports to bring understanding and cohesion to the entire team. Under well-planned conditions, these same questions and more can be the focus of discussion that team members have together.

The idea is to use the findings from the different assessment to the maximum advantage possible. By getting team members engaged in conversation about their own styles and temperaments, they increase their own Emotional Intelligence.

A Word About Personality Tests

The phrase "personality test" is a common term, but it's not the best one to use. The word "test" implies right and wrong answers, and when we consider human thinking styles, behaviors, and values, it's not good to associate them with the idea of being right or wrong. What personality tests really do is assess a person's preferences or tendencies on various scales or spectrums. With that in mind, the term *assessment* is more appropriate than test.

Avoiding the box

Perhaps the most common protest when talking about assessment tools is people not wanting to be put in a box. It's a valid protest. People adapt their thinking, their behavior, and their attitudes situation by situation, doing what they believe is necessary to succeed depending on the circumstances.

At the same time, people have natural tendencies—preferences—in how they respond to events throughout the day, and most of the time they operate in that mode.

An emotionally intelligent person may be aware of another person's customary mindset and temperament, but also is aware that people adapt situation by situation. A team leader with strong EQ recognizes where people are at any given moment and meets them in a way that creates the best possible environment for everyone to move forward with the team's goals.

Value the Differences

As we learn more about the people on our teams, we must be sure to do two things:

1. Recognize that everyone is different.
2. Value the differences.

If you have a good screening and hiring process, you've selected people who bring valuable yet diverse attributes to the table. Don't let that diversity become diluted. Yes, you want everyone on your team moving together toward the goals set before them, but each person has different strengths. You engage them to give their best if you regularly celebrate the value of their unique contributions.

As a production lead, Marilyn supervised a team of 20 people. After attending one of our teambuilding workshops she adopted the phrase "value the differences" as her own. It practically became her mantra, as hardly an hour went by when she wasn't heard saying it. Every time someone said something that was the least bit critical of someone else, Marilyn would pipe up with "value the differences," and point out how the person being criticized had strengths that were valuable and crucial to the team's success. Within a few short weeks the phrase "value the differences" had permeated her entire production team, with a noticeable increase in both morale and productivity.

As the team leader, you set the example. Nothing eats away at team spirit like negative comments and criticism. It's easy to criticize people who think differently, who behave differently, and who have different motivations. It takes purposeful effort to express how valuable those differences are to the team. You'll get closer to your goal of creating passion-driven teams when you openly value the differences.

Bottom line: Use assessment tools to gain insights into your team members, and use the assessment results as a springboard for conversations that foster teamwork.

Summary

➤ Emotional Intelligence is learnable.
➤ Research shows that top performers are more likely than average performers to have high EQ.

➤ Using assessments significantly increases your awareness of team members' strengths and weaknesses.

➤ Have team members review and discuss their assessment results; first with you, then with other team members.

➤ It is a team leader's responsibility to set the example in valuing differences.

Chapter 6

The Myths of Motivation

Perhaps you've accused someone of lacking motivation, or maybe you've heard someone else use that phrase. The problem? The idea that people lack motivation is bad psychology. It's a myth. If we're going to create passion-driven teams, we need a clear understanding about what drives people to do what they do.

Simply stated, the word *motivation* means "a reason to move." If you think about it, every action we take has a reason behind it. We eat when we're hungry, and we drink when we're thirsty. When it's late and we're tired, we head off to bed.

Continuing in motivational terms, when we're cold, we are *motivated* to seek warmth. If we're curious to find out what's going on in the world, we're *motivated* to find a source for news. Every action we take is driven by a desire to achieve or avoid something.

In the same way, everyone on our team has reasons for choosing his or her particular career field and for showing up to work each day. Therefore, proclaiming that someone lacks motivation is a false statement, because everyone has reasons for their actions!

One of the difficulties for managers and team leaders is that the word *motivation* has become firmly entrenched in some false, but commonly used phrases, such as:

Phil lacks motivation.

I can't seem to get Tanya motivated.

We need to find a way to motivate Sam.

The first mental shift needed in shattering the myths of motivation is acknowledging that we cannot motivate people, because people already have their own motivations inside them—their own reasons for moving. Our job as managers is to create conditions in which people's natural motivations propel them forward. If we want to call that "motivating people," that's fine, but understanding the truth of what's *really* going on opens the doors for developing passion on our teams.

The second thing we must acknowledge is this:

What holds people back from moving forward is not a lack of motivation. It is the presence of obstacles.

To elaborate, let's consider Michelle, an outside sales rep, who finds it difficult to make cold calls. Her sales are suffering as a result, and Bob, her sales manager, is starting to get on her case, saying she needs to get motivated.

Bob's first mistake is not realizing that Michelle certainly has motivation (reasons) to make cold calls—she knows full well she must make sales or she'll starve.

Additionally, if Bob adheres to the myth that she's not motivated, he might try different ways to increase her motivation. Granted, these techniques may work in the short term, but only for the short term. Artificially inflated motivation does not last long. Let's use a word picture to illustrate:

Let's equate motivation with the air pressure in the tires of Michelle's car. Michelle's tires enable her to move in the direction she wants to go. In this case, making sales.

But let's say that when Michelle turns to go down "Cold Call Lane," she encounters a rather large obstacle that her tires won't go over, so she stops.

When Bob sees she's not moving, he (wrongfully) assumes she doesn't have enough air in her tires to make it down Cold Call Lane, so he sends her to an exciting workshop where she learns how to "pump up" the tires so she can overcome any obstacle.

Michelle thoroughly enjoys the workshop, and the next day she puts so much air in her tires they become double their normal size. She rolls over the obstacle on Cold Call Lane as if she were driving a monster truck. She makes numerous sales, and everyone is happy.

Unfortunately, the enthusiasm from her workshop escapes much like air leaking slowly out of a balloon, and each day Michelle spends less time over-inflating her tires. A week later all the excitement from the workshop is gone, and her tires are back to their normal factory settings.

The problem, of course, is that the obstacle on Cold Call Lane is still there.

A week later, when Bob sees Michelle is not driving down Cold Call Lane anymore, he gets frustrated and tells her she lacks motivation. After a heated exchange in which he blames her for not even trying to be motivated, he considers letting her go.

As with so many other managers, Bob's thinking process is shrouded by the myths of motivation. To break free from these myths, let's stay with our word picture and consider the following points:

> ➤ It requires a lot of energy for Michelle to inflate her tires to an unnatural size.

> ➤ No matter how much energy Michelle burns over inflating her tires week after week, month after month, the obstacle at the beginning of Cold Call Lane is still in the road.

> ➤ If Bob and Michelle could redirect some energy and remove the obstacle on Cold Call Lane, Michelle would no longer need to over inflate her tires to an unnatural size—her natural motivations would be more than sufficient to produce the results she needs.

To reiterate, what prevents people from moving forward is not a lack of motivation, but rather the presence of obstacles.

In the realm of motivation, most obstacles we face are within us, and many are fear-based. For that reason we don't enjoy facing them. After all, who likes admitting that they have fears?

Dr. Dennis R. Rader and I wrote the book *Living Toad Free* to help people recognize their internal obstacles and find ways to eliminate them. In that book we used a toad as a humorous metaphor for an obstacle. Why? First, we're bigger than toads, so it provides a huge psychological advantage. Second, by looking at intangible thought patterns or fears as toads, we gain a clearer perspective of how to get past them, and even remove them altogether.

For motivation to flow, obstacles must be identified and removed

Any effort to "motivate" people cannot be "one-size-fits-all." Remember that managers must become students of the people on their teams. Each person thinks different, behaves different, and has different motivations. Similarly, each person also has a unique set of obstacles.

Before obstacles can be removed, they must first be identified. To create passion-driven teams, managers should help team members identify any obstacles holding them back, and then assist in removing them. It helps to recognize that fears are common obstacles. Fear is often the culprit that will slow peopl down—or worse yet, constrain their movements altogether.

Common Fears

Hundreds of different fears can prevent us from moving forward, so it would be impractical to cover every one. However, at least five fears are universal, and we can maximize the likelihood of creating thriving environments if we understand how to minimize the effects of these five fears:

1. Fear of criticism.
2. Fear of rejection.
3. Fear of failure.
4. Fear of not getting what you want.
5. Fear of losing what you have.

Let's consider these one by one:

Fear of Criticism

The pain of being criticized causes many to draw back into self-protection. Therefore, it's easy to understand why passion doesn't flow very well when managers and coworkers jump on a criticism bandwagon. When a mistake is made (and remember, everybody makes them), realize that it's done—it's over—it's past tense. No possibility exists to go back in time and change what happened. In other words, staying focused on the fact that someone made a mistake is useless.

Besides, when people make mistakes, their mental self-talk is often more damning than what others will give them. Still, there's no reason to criticize for the sake of criticizing, as it does nothing for increasing someone's passion.

Instead, if you're trying to build passion, turn mistakes into positive learning experiences and celebrate that new learning. The tone of any "constructive criticism" must be partnering, not parental. Replace scolding with compassion, and come alongside the person to identify how similar mistakes can be avoided in the future. Be sure to pepper your conversation with encouragement and confidence. Again, to build the camaraderie found on passion-driven teams, you'll need to be thinking "partnership."

As passion-driven teams emerge and mature, this mentality will permeate the team. But, in the beginning, such constructive conversations are the responsibility of the team leader. Pete was an experienced plumber who managed a team of eight. When one of his new plumbers messed up and caused a flood in the home of a customer, the company shelled out tens of thousands of dollars to repair the damage. When a few of the other team members started deriding the new plumber,

Pete was quick to ask them as a group how many had ever made mistakes. After silence filled the room, Pete reminded the group that, as a team, they had a choice to either criticize or learn from what happened. He then said, "Let's focus on the learning," and the team spent 20 minutes talking about what they could learn and things to watch out for in the future.

Objectively coaching someone through the aftermath of a mistake can be extremely difficult, especially if money has been lost, reputations have been sullied, or egos have been bruised. Team leaders must be exceptionally purposed in being constructive, not destructive. Objectivity is a must or the conversation can go south in a hurry. If you're going to build passion-driven teams, it should be clear by now that passion will not emerge from an atmosphere of criticism.

Fear of Failure.

Failure has to do with circumstances—not people. In other words, efforts may fail, but people cannot be labeled as failures, as long as they get up after a fall. Labeling people as failures implies they are incapable of getting up, and that implication is guaranteed to squelch drive and passion.

By encouraging people to keep moving after experiencing failure and continuing to trust them in their work, you are giving them faith, and faith is a powerful tool. Faith is more than mere belief. You can look at a chair and believe it will support your weight, but you demonstrate faith when you actually sit in it.

In the same way, managers and coworkers are creating the conditions for passion to emerge when they encourage people to get up and carry on after a fall, believing wholeheartedly that the person can and will succeed. People can sense when you truly believe in them or if you're just blowing smoke. Your faith in them must be genuine! Conversely, failing to offer encouragement sends a devastating message.

Deidre was a human resources liaison who helped new employees get situated after gaining employment with the high-tech firm where she worked. After five years on the job and surviving several cutbacks in the HR department, Deidre was doing the job of two people. Unfortunately, during a particularly stressful week, she made a huge blunder that embarrassed a new senior vice-president. Deidre corrected the problem right away, but for months afterward, every time she bumped into that VP, he furled his brow in disgust. It was so intense that Deidre began losing confidence. Worse yet, her favorite assignments were being delegated to others, without so much as a conversation as to why.

Never was anything said about her gaffe, but at the same time, not even the HR manager offered Deidre any words of encouragement. After a few months of the standoffish atmosphere, Deidre was ready to throw in the towel. She didn't feel that people trusted her judgment anymore; she even stopped trusting herself.

Obviously, neither the HR manager nor the VP were concerned about creating passion-driven teams. Encourage people to get up after a fall and trust them to perform the job for which they were hired. Yes, some coaching and correction may be needed, but by encouraging and trusting, you're creating conditions for confidence to remain (or re-emerge), and for passion to flow.

Fear of Rejection

Whereas failure has to do with circumstances, rejection is personal. Human beings, by their very design, are social creatures. The most calloused individuals may say they don't care what people think, but the truth is that there is always someone in their lives whose opinion matters.

Most employees care about what their bosses and coworkers think. Therefore, it's not a good idea to flat out reject ideas from your team members, even if you don't think a particular idea will work. Do you want your team members to continue growing, contributing, and being creative? Then be cautious of how you say no to ideas.

Think about when you've offered up ideas: You've given them thought. You've considered how your ideas benefit the team or the project, and you're convinced they will truly help. If, when you start explaining your ideas, your supervisor brushes you off without hearing all the details, the rejection can be painful. Even if you learn a suggestion truly won't work, being on the receiving end of rejection still hurts. The ripple effect? You're not as fast to offer up an idea the next time. I've seen entire teams shut down because of how the leader says no to ideas. That's going the wrong direction if you're trying to build a passion-driven team.

As a team leader, think carefully about how your actions and words will be perceived. Besides, rather than dismiss an idea out of hand, you might actually learn something that makes the team or the project better.

This very thing happened to Marty, a manager at an electrical engineering firm that specialized in creating high-end, customized solutions for their clients. At a staff meeting that included the company president, two outside consultants, and the vice president of marketing, Marty made the mistake of too quickly rejecting an idea from someone on his team.

Sarah, an up-and-coming engineer, had proposed creating scaled-back, standardized solutions they could sell to smaller clients with a minimal amount of effort. Because Marty held great pride in the firm's ability to customize its solutions, his first reaction was to vigorously defend the brand without even considering her idea. Sarah seemed to shut down, but a level of tension filled the room.

Toward the end of the meeting, Marty apologized for the abruptness of his reaction, but despite Marty's apology, Sarah still felt slighted and rejected. In the end, her suggestions were actually implemented and Sarah was placed in charge of an entirely new industry group. However, it took much time and effort on Marty's part to rebuild a trusting relationship with Sarah.

Can you see how easy it is to lose trust? It takes a long time to earn it, but only a few seconds to lose it. Be careful how you respond to your team's ideas.

Fear of Not Getting What You Want

"Wants" are motivators—reasons to move. When people are afraid of not getting what they want, their behavior can take several distinct routes.

In some cases, this particular fear leads to people not taking any action at all. Such would be the case if Michelle, our salesperson who wasn't making cold calls, was afraid of not getting a sale.

It could be that she wanted a sale, but was afraid she wouldn't get one, so she didn't even try. Her inaction also could have been based in a fear of rejection. Both fears can produce call-reluctance in salespeople.

One way to help people overcome the fear of not getting what they want is to identify a positive if the "want" is not achieved. For instance, in the case of salespeople afraid of hearing no, sales managers have been known to implement "no" contests.

Example: After getting a dozen confirmed "no" responses, the salesperson is rewarded with an appealing incentive. This turns a negative into a positive, and actually transforms the fear into something fun—plus it keeps the salesperson making calls.

Identifying a positive was also the way that Jolene's coworkers convinced her to apply for a supervisory position. Jolene maintains a low-profile, but was well-qualified for the supervisor opening. She wasn't going to apply for the job because she didn't think she would get it.

Her coworkers pointed out that even if someone else got the position, senior management would become aware of Jolene's capabilities and she would then be on their radar. Turns out her coworkers were right. Jolene didn't get that particular position, but management placed her on the "management fast track," and she was offered the very next supervisory position that opened up.

By the way, notice how Jolene's teammates encouraged her—the spark of a passion-driven team!

Although the fear of not getting what you want leads some people to inaction, it leads other people to become more active, but not in a positive way. Some display a "sour grapes" or fatalistic attitude that casts a dark cloud over all those around them. Others may go so far as throwing a tantrum or even intimidating others so they can have their way.

This is not the action one finds in a person who's trying to be on a passion-driven team, but when this happens, team leaders must remain objective. Chris had a situation like this when she was managing a supermarket. One of her management trainees was afraid of not getting selected for the next assistant manager opening. He began lobbying coworkers and was even making comments to customers about why he should be selected. When Chris heard what was going on, she met with the trainee and pulled out the job description for the assistant manager position. With an attitude of partnering, she went over each job responsibility with him line-by-line, and together they assessed where he stood on each item. By the end of the meeting they had created a specific development plan together. The trainee saw what he still needed to learn before he could be promoted. He also became a huge fan of Chris because of the way she treated him.

It would have been easy for Chris to tell the young man to "clam up" or "knock it off." Instead, she invested a bit of time, and built an ally.

Obviously, we can't give our employees everything they want. But part of being the leader of a passion-driven team means listening to people and finding appropriate ways to help them achieve their desires. If it is impossible to give someone what they want, tactfully educating them about what is needed to make it happen or explaining why it can't happen is always better than a blunt "no."

Fear of Losing What You Have

What people possess gives them a sense of security. Possessions can be tangible (tools, desks, cars) or intangible (position, authority, respect), and the presence of those things helps people stay engaged and productive. When making decisions, managers do well to consider what a person "has" and therefore "has to lose." If someone must lose something for the good of the company, try to identify a counter balance.

Such was not the case for some nurses working for a home health agency in the Midwest. Already carrying heavy patient loads, a number of nurses originally hired as hourly employees were given salaried positions. This enabled the employer to actually lower the amount they paid these nurses while increasing their case load. Moreover, these nurses were forced to be "on call" 24 hours a day. When several of the nurses went to management to discuss being put back on an hourly wage, they were not only denied, but management also threatened to rescind some of their benefits if they pursued the matter.

Suffice it to say that morale for this team of nurses hit rock bottom in no time, and turnover increased from 10 percent to more than 30 percent in less than a year. People feared losing control of their lives as burnout swept through the organization.

This particular management team got it wrong, because in order to create passion-driven teams, we want to minimize fears, not create them. In many ways, managing people who fear losing what they have has parallels working with those who fear not getting what they want: some become more reserved, but others speak out more.

Here's a guide for when change occurs or the loss of something is inevitable: The fear of loss can be offset by the hope of a gain elsewhere. This can take time and effort, but if you are genuine about wanting to accommodate someone's concerns, they sense the value you are placing on their perspective, and that comes back to you. Again, it's just too easy to blow people off. Investing yourself into your team members serves to keep their passions engaged.

Motivation vs. Manipulation

Remember those false, but commonly used phrases we looked at earlier? They're all too common. Picture two managers talking about one of their employees:

"I wish we could find a way to motivate Jack."
"Yeah, me too. He's not getting into this new program."
"If only we could figure out how to get him engaged."

As we've discussed, employees cannot be motivated, because they are *already* motivated. They already have reasons for doing what they do, and if someone is not engaging with the team, the manager must do one or both of the following:

➤ Identify a person's natural motivations and connect them to the tasks at hand.

➤ Identify and remove whatever obstacles are in the way of the person's natural motivations.

Because motivation is commonly misunderstood, many managers mistakenly believe they are motivating people, when in reality they are manipulating them. Essentially, it's manipulation when we think of a reason others should do something and then convince them of our correctness. This does nothing to engage a person's passions.

To truly "motivate" someone (using the colloquial term), we must create conditions in which employees engage for reasons that are important to *them*.

A few years back a large corporation put out a call for proposals on how to roll out their new strategic plan so employees would embrace it. I learned that one proposal included surveying some of the employees to find out what was important to them. Then, working with employees throughout the corporate strata, they would look for ways to connect the values identified in the survey to the main points in the strategic plan. A presentation would then be created that included, among other things, how the employees' values connected with the action items in the strategic plan.

Senior management thought the survey was an unnecessary step, and they chose a different route.

A few months later, when I was training at one of this company's manufacturing plants, I was approached by a number of people telling me that "corporate came out and gave us a seminar" about how the strategic plan would be good for the *company*. "Nothing in their plan addressed any of our concerns as employees," they said. "It's all about the company and *their* profitability—not us."

Interestingly, I was there training on a different topic. The fact that these employees brought it up meant it was a serious issue for them!

On passion-driven teams, everyone on the team subscribes deeply to the team's vision, mission, values, and strategies. The corporate office at this particular company was not yet in tune with the fact that people will engage a vision for their own reasons—not because they hear it preached from an ivory tower.

Granted, these employees were not seeing that they were part of the company, yet obviously something deeper was going on. Senior management failed to create the conditions in which people wanted to engage for their own reasons. As a result, people weren't taking personal ownership of the plan—it was just another edict from the ivory tower.

We have control over the conditions we create, not what drives people internally

The basic truth connecting motivation and passion is this: If we create conditions that connect to people's internal motivators and value systems, employees engage. But if we create conditions that clash with people's value systems, employees disengage. It's just that simple.

If you doubt me, try getting a Republican to volunteer at Democratic headquarters or a Democrat to volunteer at Republican headquarters. Because political parties are, in essence, value systems, people are drawn to organizations that most closely align with their values, and stay away from organizations that don't.

This is not to say that we can't work with people who hold different value systems—quite the contrary. John and Wendy are worlds apart politically, but at the dental office where they work, both are fervent evangelists for oral hygiene and superior patient care. John and Wendy decided to study passion-driven teams and, before long, the entire office staff was onboard. Every person genuinely cares about each patient and the experience that person has at the dentist's office.

John started by showing his coworkers the office vision and mission statements and asking people how it related to them personally. He wasn't in their face, it was just a conversation. Then, when Wendy kept up the conversations by talking about people's answers, the bonds grew and people took ownership, with the vision and mission statements serving as a central hub.

I love this example, because it so clearly shows people supporting an organization's vision, mission, and values for their own reasons. Our job is to create the conditions in which people feel they are contributing something *they* want to contribute, and getting something back *they* want in return.

To bring out people's passion, you need to:

➤ become an ardent student of what motivates people from within.

➤ create a safe environment in which people feel welcome to engage and valued for doing so.

Maintaining a win/win mindset

No matter what your industry, work must be accomplished and employees must be engaged in the work. Something else you can adopt to help these two come together is a win/win mindset. According to best-selling author Stephen Covey in his book *Seven Habits of Highly Effective People*, win/win thinking has two components:

1. *Courage* to stand up for our own convictions.
2. *Consideration* for the other party's wants and needs.

Unfortunately, in their effort to translate the goals they must accomplish, many managers mishandle the consideration part of Covey's equation. After all, truly seeking out and considering another person's point of view takes time and effort. In its place, managers presume to know other people's dreams and desires, and just like the corporation that mishandled rolling out is strategic plan, managers often try telling their teams how a particular action is going to benefit them.

The problem? They genuinely believe that they've given consideration to the wants and needs of their team. It may be a well-intended thought process, but it misses the boat. We must seek and understand other people's points of view—from their own words, not our own imaginings.

The easiest way to discover what employees want is to ask! This seems like common sense, but, if it is, why do we still have managers standing by water coolers trying to figure out ways to get someone motivated?

Covey's action item for *consideration* is "seeking first to understand." Ken, a manager who decided he was going to start thinking "win/win," had a tough time with this. He sat by himself in his office thinking about his workers' needs, and then decided how he would adapt his new plans to fit those needs. In his mind, he was "seeking first to understand."

You can guess the problem that ensued. When Ken went to implement his ideas, his people were less than enthusiastic. He even got defensive when they told him he wasn't considering their needs. From Ken's perspective, he *had*. But from their perspective, he hadn't asked their input—he only *assumed* he knew what they wanted.

The truth? No matter how well-intended, Ken's approach was not win/win. He never took the time to ask. In fact, his technique was more like manipulating, not motivating.

Therefore, use these definitions and you'll be better equipped at developing teams that are passion-driven:

➤ Manipulation is thinking of reasons others will want to do something, and then convincing them of your correctness.

➤ Motivation is genuinely seeking out someone else's wants, needs, and desires, and then finding mutually agreeable solutions, so that both their goals and your own goals are met.

Summary

➤ Everyone already has motivation—their own reasons for moving.

➤ What slows people down or stops them altogether is not lack of motivation, but the presence of obstacles.

➤ Rather than having people waste energy by artificially inflating their motivation, help them identify the obstacles and find ways to remove them.

➤ Genuinely learn what other people want, then find mutually agreeable methods that allow both their goals and your goals to be met.

Chapter 7

The Power of Water Cooler Conversations

Day after day, Rick shows up to work. And, day after day, he works hard. He likes his work, he's paid well, and he gets along well with coworkers. But Rick is considering looking for work elsewhere. Why?

Because Rick doesn't have a clue about what direction his company is heading.

Practically everyone where Rick works is kept in the dark about the company's medium and long-term goals. Rick asks his boss about it from time to time, but he's routinely waived off and his commitment is starting to wear thin.

Rick wants what most workers want: to understand how his work contributes to the big picture.

What Rick might like is something that Jerri experiences on a regular basis. Jerri is a junior high school math teacher, and she feels totally plugged in and fully aware of what's going on at her school and how her work factors in. The reason? Her principal makes it a practice to talk with teachers informally throughout the week. Sometimes it's in the hallway while students are arriving for school. Other times it's a chat in the cafeteria during lunch, or maybe near the end of the day after the students have gone home.

The point is that both her principal and the vice principal make the effort to touch base with the staff and faculty several times a week and keep them informed about things that are of interest to them. The result? People feel included. They feel "in the loop." They are engaged with what's going on.

Jerri's principal is someone I would consider to be a pro at holding effective water cooler conversations.

What Is a Water Cooler Conversation?

Water cooler conversations get their name because of how people gather informally around the water cooler at work to discuss topics of interest. Sometimes the conversations are nothing but small talk, but sometimes they can also be about things that matter.

In the effort to build passion-driven teams, water cooler conversations are a powerful way to keep people connected.

When people on passion-driven teams have water cooler conversations, it's a time to share learning, communicate faith in one another, give feedback on various projects, or even reconnect with the big picture of what they're trying to accomplish.

This last factor is a vital component to the creation of passion-driven teams. On passion-driven teams, people enthusiastically subscribe to their team's purpose, and everyone is well aware of how the purpose ties to the organization's vision, mission, and values.

This should tell you why passion-driven teams are rather rare. Too many team leaders (and many organizations in general) do a horrible job of sharing the big picture with their employees.

When the big picture is a no show

Unfortunately, the problem of not communicating the big picture is more universal than you might think. Research from KEYGroup, an executive coaching company, found that nearly half of all employees do not have clearly defined goals, nor do they receive feedback on their performance more than once a week. Robert Kaplan and David Norton, authors of *Execution Premium: Linking Strategy to Operations for Competitive Advantage*, found that "A mere 7 percent of employees today fully understand their company's business strategies and what's expected of them in order to help achieve company goals."

Clearly, people need to be brought into the loop on the direction of your company or you'll have a tough time developing passion on your teams. It should be common sense: When employees understand the goals of their company and how their actions align with those goals, those employees are more productive—and their company is more profitable.

Conversely, nature abhors a vacuum. When no clear goals exist, or when they're not publicized so that people can subscribe to them and promote them, individual missions and visions tend to rise up and compete with each other. In other words, people start promoting their own agendas. The result is unnecessary conflict, delays, and lost revenue, all because of turf wars that consume valuable time and energy.

The danger of fluff

You're also going to have a tough time connecting your teams to company goals if your organization's mission statement is fluffy or over generalized. Hopefully the following useless mission statement is nothing like yours:

> Our commitment to seeking integrated solutions and staying on schedule will benefit our end users with a positive return on their investment.

It may *sound* important, but it says nothing.

To learn what kind of advantage you can have by ensuring your team is plugged into a clear, succinct, organizational mission, walk into any business and find their mission statement hanging on a wall. Take note of its meanings, and then survey any five employees you meet from that company. Ask if they know their company's mission.

Chances are you'll either hear five different responses, or the ever-popular "I don't know." Some people may even laugh at you, but most likely you'll realize that if your team was focused on a clear, succinct mission, it would generate momentum and give you an advantage over the competition.

If you don't have a clear mission statement for your organization or your team, visit *www.passiondriventeams.com* for detailed instructions on how to create one.

Does a company need a mission statement to function? Obviously not. The mere fact that so many companies survive without them answers that question. But a well-written mission statement to which everyone subscribes increases a team's ability to focus and makes it easier for work to flow. In other words, your team can thrive instead of survive.

People must be included

I like what Paul Johnson of Shortcuts to Results, LLC, says: "Motivation depends on having a clear path to accomplishing a desired result. It's okay if every detail is not in place and a few variables exist, but the path to success must not be shrouded in fog."

Joanne G. Sujansky, CEO and founder of KEYGroup, and author of *Keeping the Millennials*, holds a similar opinion. Sujansky offers excellent advice for leaders and managers: "Continually communicate with your employees and state your expectations of them. Tell them what you want, what they did right, what you expect of them, and how you will measure their progress. Share the organizational vision and goals so employees understand the big picture. Realize that your team members want to know where the organization is going and how that direction affects their personal objectives."

About the Human Brain

For many, being introduced to company goals and mission statements will be like a breath of fresh air. For others, it may represent a change in their habits and comfort zones. But for success in creating passion-driven teams, we must introduce people to regularly thinking about the big picture and how it ties to our vision, mission, and values.

If you've previously struggled with getting people to embrace something they've not done before, it's probably because the methods you used clashed with how the human brain functions. However, good news is upon us: Recent discoveries in how the brain operates have given us valuable insights for engaging people to both modify their habits and move together in a common direction.

Leaning heavily on the work of research psychiatrist Jeffrey Schwartz and executive coach David Rock, we need to pause and think about why it's so hard to change people's habits.

For example, despite being presented with facts on how a change will be beneficial, the majority of people fight against the change, even if they know it's in their own best interest.

The reason has to do with what we might call "hard-wired neurons." Change is not just a matter of deciding to do something differently. Any attempt to modify our habits literally requires a change in the physiology of the brain. Here's why: To maintain efficiency, our brains create "hard-wired" cells with the sole function of making our habits and routine behaviors easy.

Think about it. When driving a car, you hardly think about the steps necessary to open the door, insert the key, and put the car in gear. Yet within a matter of moments you're cruising down the road. Through repetition and over time, these behaviors became hard-wired, so they don't require very much conscious thought.

It wasn't that way when you first learned to drive through. For example, if you drive a stick shift, you probably remember quite a few stalls and jerky starts. But there came a time when you found yourself sailing along in fourth gear and don't remember shifting to get there.

That's the power of hard-wired neurons. When the brain notices you do something regularly, it creates highly efficient neuron cells that are programmed with the knowledge needed for that activity. This frees up your conscious, critical-thinking process, which is electro-chemical in nature and highly energy-intensive.

The high levels of energy needed for critical thinking are evidenced by the fact that we can feel extremely tired after doing nothing but making decisions all day.

Water Cooler Conversations

By now you may be asking what all this has to do with engaging people to work together passionately toward common goals. The answer has to do with how we present those goals and how we talk about them in our day-to-day conversations.

The power of informal communication is often overlooked. Business communication classes teach proper voice mail and e-mail etiquette, as well as how to write memos, letters, and proposals, but they gloss over the power of informal communication.

However, by relying on some powerful findings from neuroscience research and the writings of Rock and Schwartz, you can help your team achieve consistent, sustained top performance, all reinforced by simple water cooler conversations. To do this you'll need to learn about three things:

1. Focus
2. Expectation
3. Attention density

Focus

A person's focus is extremely powerful. Consider the phrase "that which you focus on you get more of." The brain pays attention to your experiences, your thoughts, your insights, your fears, and so on. Clearly focusing your attention on something stabilizes brain circuitry, similar to how hard-wired neurons remember your physical habits, such as driving a car.

When creating passion-driven teams, getting people focused involves painting a desirable picture of the future. Usually done with word pictures, the idea is to give your team a mental image of what you want, not what you don't want. Remember, mental circuitry resists being changed once it's in place, so be sure to clarify the mental picture of what you want.

Did you ever try to get someone to do something by telling him what you didn't want him to do? The story that made the biggest impact on me regarding the importance of proper focus has to with one of the best pitchers in the history of Major League Baseball history, Warren Spahn. In game four of the 1957 World Series, Spahn was one out away from winning the game for his team, the Milwaukee Braves. It was the top of the ninth and the Braves were ahead 4 to 1, but two men were on base for the New York Yankees, and respected slugger Elston Howard was at the plate with a full count.

Spahn's manager, apparently trying to break the tension, called "time" and came out to the mound. The only thing he said was, "Whatever you do, don't throw him a high outside pitch." After he returned to the dugout, the only words flashing through Spahn's mind were "high" and "outside." And that was the next pitch Spahn threw. Howard swung on it for a home run and tied the game.

Although the Braves eventually went on to win the game and the series itself, Spahn shared this story with many groups throughout the years, questioning why anyone would ever motivate another person to do something by giving them a mental picture of what they didn't want.

At water cooler conversations, you want focus. Talk about what you want—not what you don't want.

Expectation

Secondly, we must engage the power of expectation. The simple truth is that people see what they expect to see. Consider two executives: One sees workers primarily as lazy, while the other sees them as desiring to do their best. Each one will look for—and see—behaviors that validate their expectations.

If people do not see what they're expecting, the brain perceives an "error," and often communicates that error as a feeling of fear. Because people don't like being in error or being in fear, they often look very hard to see what they want to see—even if it isn't there! Naturally, this is counterproductive.

We've already learned that fear is a common obstacle to forward movement, so, as team leaders, we must create the conditions for people to be open to new things.

A great way to reverse the brain's tendency to think "error" and communicate fear is to have people explore possibilities outside of their expectations. Think of it as helping them realize it's okay to be pleasantly surprised if they don't see what they expect. In other words, it's okay to have an "a-ha" moment—an insight that changes their attitude or perspective about something.

Shannon is a regional sales manager for a cellular telephone company, and she refers to this concept as simply being open to new possibilities. "I teach my team to be on the lookout for new ways to make things happen, and not to get stuck doing only what they've done before. Yes, we have rules and guidelines we must follow, but blessed are the flexible."

The key in encouraging open expectation is to let people see things with fresh eyes on their own terms. People won't believe things are different just because you say so.

Encourage people to look at things differently on their own. The ideas that get generated will amaze you.

Attention density

Finally, the part that ties everything together is attention density. The term refers to the amount of attention given to a particular subject over time. Attention density is one of the reasons executive coaching is so effective. A one-day training workshop puts you face-to-face with the material for eight hours straight. But if you learn the same material one hour a week for eight weeks, your mind has not only stabilized its mental circuits on the subject (focus), it has also had more time to recognize and own the "a-ha" insights that have emerged (expectation). The result of learning through time is you'll retain and internalize a much higher percentage of the subject matter.

If you think about it, these three components can be factored into informal, water cooler conversations.

1. You can mention the big picture (focus).
2. You can talk about new insights (expectation).
3. You can do it often, and do it informally (attention density).

Whether you bump into someone in the break room, down the hall, or actually at the water cooler, as the team leader you can ask people for their feedback and thoughts on various topics. Here's a question that might catch people off guard, but I'll guarantee you it will affect their focus and their expectation: "What do you think we could be doing more of to achieve our mission and vision?"

You can also talk about new insights other people have had, and ask if they have any suggestions for helping the team move in the direction of its goals.

Naturally, water cooler conversations have a few downsides. First, some people won't catch all they should, because these aren't "regular meetings." Also, make sure you never discipline or correct anyone at such a "meeting." No gossip, either; water cooler conversations are for positive, growth-focused topics only!

Not only are water cooler conversations powerful for capturing ideas, learning, and building commitment, but they also allow you to take advantage of the brain's normal functioning to reinforce your own passion—as well as that of your team members. Thirsty yet?

Summary

➤ A majority of people do not understand how their work contributes to the bigger picture.

➤ Even fewer people know the direction their company is going.

➤ Because of how the brain works, it can be difficult to get people unstuck from long-held habits.

➤ Informal conversations can energize people toward common goals if those conversations:

◆ Are framed with a big picture of the expected end result.

◆ Encourage people to look for and expect new insights.

◆ Are consistent and ongoing.

Chapter 8

The Do's and Don'ts of Delegating

Jason let out a heavy sigh. "There is so much to do," he thought to himself. "I wish I could assign someone else to this project, but it is too important. I need to make sure this gets done right."

"You can't do everything yourself," he heard someone say. Jason looked up from his desk to see his friend Mark standing in the doorway of his office. Mark was a confident man in his late 20s. His department of 25 people seemed to run like clockwork. Just last month they had been recognized for being the most profitable department in the company, achieving a 23 percent margin. Every other department was struggling to meet the minimum goal of 7 percent.

"How's it going, Jason?" Mark asked, as he flashed a sympathetic, but concerned smile.

Jason leaned back in his chair. "Well, I'm working 10, sometimes 12-hour days, and I'm here six days a week," he replied. "I'm missing deadlines and my employees don't seem to care. They take off as soon as it hits five o'clock."

Hopefully Jason's situation doesn't sound familiar. However, if you're relating to him, it's probably time to become a student of the do's and don'ts of delegation.

In the simplest of terms, delegation is dividing a big picture into an appropriate number of puzzle pieces and then assigning the work associated with those pieces to others.

Obviously, there's a lot more to it, because delegation has many facets and levels, so let's take a closer look.

In one way, delegating is like being a translator. When leadership is flying at 40,000 feet they've got the big picture in front of them. They're looking around at the forests and looking out at the horizon. After deciding the best direction for the company, leaders set goals and communicate those goals to the managers.

Managers must not only be able to interpret those goals accurately, they must be able to translate them and dice them up into specific action items for the front-line employees working in the middle of the forest amongst the trees. Making those assignments can't just be "here—do this." People on passion-driven teams want to see how their work contributes to the big picture.

Finding a balance when communicating between leadership and front-line employees can be a difficult job. After all, many leaders forget what it's like to work among the trees, and most front-line employees have not been up in the leadership airplane, looking around at 40,000 feet. For that matter, most managers do not spend much time in the leadership airplane, either. Still, they must understand the mindsets and requests coming at them from both directions.

If managers do not learn how to translate goals into specific puzzle pieces and assign to others the work related to those pieces, the system backs up in relatively short order. This is why it's so important that managers and team leaders leave behind the mindset of being a front-line employee.

This was the difference between Jason and Mark. For whatever reason, Jason never relinquished the hands-on, technical work he loved doing. Because of that, in spite of being promoted to management, he never became a student of what it means to delegate.

Mark was also a talented, exceptional front-line employee. But, when he got promoted, he realized right away that he needed to know the strengths and weaknesses of the people on his team so he could delegate effectively. To learn these things Mark spent time with each team member. It wasn't very formal: he just spent time talking with them, and along the way he found out what they liked and didn't like about their jobs. He gave them training if they needed special knowledge or skills. But he also took time to learn the art of delegation. Yes, he stepped in when help was needed, but he didn't fall back to his old responsibilities.

What you delegate, to whom you delegate, and how you delegate can make a huge difference in whether you create passion-driven teams, or teams offering only grudging compliance.

What you can delegate

Hundreds of books already tell you what tasks and duties you should delegate, and which ones you should do yourself. Those will change from company to company and job to job, so we won't take up space replicating those lists here (although we've resourced a practical list for you on *www.passiondriventeams.com*). Instead, let's talk about the mental aspect of delegation.

Essentially, when you delegate, you should be transferring (or sharing) three things:

1. Responsibility (the burden or obligation to complete the work).
2. Authority (the power or control to do the work).
3. Accountability (the obligation to explain and justify the results).

People's passions are fueled when they can "own" what they do. If you fail to transfer any of these three ingredients, you minimize personal ownership.

To whom you delegate

Felix Dennis, founder of *Maxim* and chairman of Dennis Publishing, wrote a great article on delegating, which he titled "Hand It Over!" According to Dennis, "It's so easy to delegate important work to, or promote, people who are similar to you in temperament and skill sets. So easy and so wrong."

As with Mark's example, we must know the capabilities and limitation of the people on our teams. Through simple, informal conversations, you can ask people what they want to learn and where they feel most confident. You can ask a lot more, but you should know at least that much about people before you start delegating to them.

In addition to someone's knowledge base and skill sets, you can also observe a person's behavioral style. For example, what is a person's communication preference? Does a person like a lot of detail or just bullet points? How does a person solve problems? Interact with people? Deal with pressure? Follow rules? When delegating, you need to know who is capable of what.

As Andrew Carnegie said, "The secret to success is not in doing your own work, but in recognizing the right man to do it." (In our day, I'm sure Andrew would say "person.")

How you delegate

When you delegate, you should be especially careful to do five things:

1. Think through the big picture and decide the best way to split it up into its various puzzle pieces.

2. Carefully match work with the best people to do it.
3. Explain face-to-face how the work they'll be doing contributes to the big picture.
4. Come to an agreement on what constitutes a finished product.
5. Follow up.

Jason struggled (and so did his team) because of how he delegated. He didn't spend much time analyzing the big picture and dividing it up in ways that could be matched to people's strengths.

That led to people getting assignments that didn't align with their passions or interests.

Between that and Jason not always explaining how the work fit into the company's goals, people weren't exactly fired up about what they were doing. As you can imagine, that led to mediocre efforts.

Although Jason almost always gave people responsibility, authority, and accountability, it wasn't long before the mediocre work he was seeing during his follow-up meetings led him to take back the authority over the project (the control of the work). The result? With Jason re-assuming control over the work, his team members felt no ownership of it, and therefore no need to justify the results. That's why they were out the door at five o'clock.

Piecing It All Together

As we learn from the examples of both Mark and Jason, analyzing the big picture and dividing up the work appropriately sets the tone for everything else. Things to keep in mind when analyzing include:

> ➤ What is the expected end result of the overall project, and when is it due?

> Who is available, and what are their capabilities, limitations, and preferences?

> What are those people's current workloads?

Next, think like a puzzle-solver. Consider people's knowledge, skill sets, and temperaments, and divide the work into reasonable chunks that can be matched to people with the skills and temperaments that fit best. Obviously, undesirable tasks must still get done, but by spreading these out, people won't feel dumped on.

When meeting with the people to whom you are going to delegate, some will have an innate understanding of what you're asking them to do, while others will need more guidance. In either case, you'll still want to explain the overarching goals and tasks, and have a good description of the expected end result. By no means should you tell them exactly how to do it. For them to "own" the project, you want their input.

How to truly transfer ownership

When delegating to someone for the first time or for someone who might demonstrate lower innate ownership of the work, first explain the project, and then ask them to spend time outlining what they think will be required for the project to succeed. This is not something they do "on the spot," but rather in their own private planning session.

The outline they create should include:

> a description of the end result as they understand it.

> the resources they think they'll need (personnel, tools, finances, technology, software, and so on).

> any learning they believe must occur.

> what safety concerns they may have.

➤ what kind of coordination with other departments might be needed (if any).

➤ what milestones should serve as checkpoints.

➤ anything else they believe to be pertinent to the successful completion of the project.

Ask people to genuinely spend some time with this and then come back to you relatively soon to review it. Face-to-face meetings will work best, because two-thirds of our communication is body language. Tell them you're not asking for a complete project plan, but merely an outline created by them about what they'll be doing.

When reviewing their outline, if you see they are missing major aspects of the project, raise those points and ask them to take their overview back and rework it. Once they're within 85 –90 percent of where you think they should be, agree on some follow-up dates to check progress. You'll want to make sure you clarify the type of information you'll be looking for at those meetings, and, by all means, hold to those dates!

Different types of delegation

Obviously, not all delegation requires this much effort. Simpler tasks can be delegated with relative quickness and ease. Best-selling author Stephen Covey divides delegation into two basic categories: *gopher* delegation and *stewardship* delegation.

Gopher delegation requires very little thought or planning. You simply tell people "go for this" or "go for that." But being a "delegatee" in gofer delegation doesn't require much thought, either.

Such delegation has its place (albeit limited), but it provides few benefits for professional development or fueling anyone's passions. Besides, gofer delegation is a first cousin to micromanaging.

What we've been talking about in this chapter is steward-ship delegation, because it involves giving people total stew-ardship (responsibility, authority, and accountability) over a project. It requires much more time and patience, but the ben-efits far outweigh the cost.

Do's and Don'ts From Respected Delegators

In my training and consulting work, I've encountered many team leaders who delegate extremely well (Mark among them). A few years back I surveyed some of these well-respected delegators to learn what they thought was important for suc-cessful delegating. Most of the content in this chapter is based on their feedback. And, while it would be impractical to list every idea and tip they provided, here are some thoughts you might find helpful:

Delegate that which is possible

! Find the right person for the job.
Delegating to the wrong person can spell disaster.

! Teach/educate your employees where needed.
Equipping others builds their value and minimizes their fears.

! Don't expect perfection or overreact to mistakes.
Mistakes mean learning occurred; finger-pointing kills passion.

Angela says she always double checks to see if the task she's delegating is appropriate for the person getting the as-signment. "If it's not, you're setting the person up to fail," she says. "When that happens, you get more than a failed task. You get a disgruntled employee, and the failure affects everyone on the team." Angela advocates ongoing training, so that as people learn more, they can handle more complex projects. Mark says that when he delegates, he always asks people where they think they might have problems along the way. "If what they tell me sounds like it could slow the project down, I locate a resource who can help in that area."

Build trust

> **:** Address any worry or concerns people have.
> *When they know you care, they remain committed.*
> **:** Trust people—and allow them to make mistakes.
> *Mistakes are usually fixable—plus, people learn from them.*
> **:** Don't expect them to do things like you would.
> *Delegate for results, not processes.*

Robert says delegation always involves trust. "Training people is part of the delegating job," he says, "but there comes a time when you just give them a project and let them run with it." Robert also says that in addition to trusting people with authority, sometimes you're trusting them with your career, so you want to make sure you do a good job in the delegating process.

Bill builds trust by first delegating small projects to new employees. He wants to see how they work and if they can do a good job. As success occurs, Bill delegates increasingly larger projects.

Give the big picture

> **:** Agree on the definition and deadline for the end product.
> *What does success look like and when do you need it?*

Scott says nothing causes more mistakes or more frustration than someone being assigned a project without knowing how their work fits in with the big picture. "Always clearly communicate how the task or project furthers the larger goal."

Mary agrees: "If people don't see how their work is part of a bigger picture, the decisions they make along the way can create problems and extra work later on." With everything else being equal, if people have two options before them and one option leads to a better end result for the overarching goal, they can make the better choice if they have the big picture.

Take your hands off the project

❢ Don't step in and take over (rare exceptions exist here).
  Instead, study how to be a better delegator.

❢ Don't give people responsibility without authority.
  People need the ability to make their own decisions.

❢ Offer to help only if things get crazy.
  Extra hands are sometimes needed—just don't take over!

❢ Give encouragement.
  People want to know you believe in them.

Jim says, "Understand that delegating is not the same as doing something yourself. If you expect the person to be a psychic who anticipates your every move, then you aren't delegating, you're looking for a clone." Jim says that a huge benefit of delegating is people gaining skills along the way, and that's more likely to happen when you "let others put their own stamp on a project or task."

Scott says that delegating without getting input from the person taking on the project is either "gopher delegation" or micromanagement. He also says that people take more ownership of a project when we "delegate with value." That means we should "ask how the task or project will further the person's skills and learning. When you can align that with the person's career and development goals, their commitment levels go way up."

Robert says, "Often, the people to whom I delegate don't do things the way I would. Still, their outcomes are usually successful—and often more successful than if things had been done my way!"

Get "repeat back"

: Meet face-to-face if at all possible.
More than two-thirds of communication is non-verbal.

: Agree on milestones.
Regular "checkups" minimize the likelihood of surprises at the end.

: Don't ask, "Do you understand?"
You need confirmation. Have them repeat back their understanding.

: Keep your appointments for follow-ups.
Blowing off these appointments says you don't care.

Lisa M. says that delegation requires good communication. "Make sure the person who's taking on the project can explain back to you their perception of what's required." You want to know you're both on the same page.

Monica J. says it's important to "get feedback right away," and to "clear up any miscommunications before they occur."

Jim B. agrees. "You are never as clear as you think you are." He also says to make sure there's an agreement on deadlines, and what kind of feedback you expect along the way.

Give credit

: Acknowledge initiative and problem-solving.
If you give thanks for these things, you get more of them.

? Speak well of your team members' work in front of others.

Words get around, and your positive words build their team pride.

? Don't take credit for someone else's work.

If you want your team to flourish, give your team the credit they deserve.

Sonya M. says she never wants her people to feel taken for granted. She not only praises them in one-on-one conversations, but she points out how their work contributes to team and organizational goals in meetings. "I make sure I'm very specific," says Sonya. "Saying 'great job' doesn't cut it. I also give people a chance to give their own comments. Sometimes they'd like their coworkers to know something that I may leave out."

Bill S. says, "For a delegated task to be successful, people need to be able to put their signature on it and get credit for it."

Scott H. holds the same opinion. He adds that even if the project was originally delegated to you, "if portions of the project were completed through you delegating them to someone else, be sure to delegate the recognition, too."

Summary

➤ You can't do everything yourself—that's why you're on a team.

➤ Managers must translate goals into "puzzle pieces"—strong planning skills are required.

➤ The puzzle pieces get assigned to people who have the best match for the work.

➤ When delegating, delegate everything: responsibility, authority, and accountability.

➤ Transfer ownership appropriately based on the delegate, and don't take it back.

➤ Ensure people understand how the work contributes to the big picture.

➤ Keep appropriate communication flowing back forth, and keep appointments.

➤ Give credit.

Chapter 9

Maintaining a Balanced Diet of Meetings

This chapter is not about how to run meetings—many other books on the market can tell you how to do that. Instead, we'll be considering how to determine the value of meetings so that you can maintain a "balanced diet" in a way that keeps your team healthy and active.

When talking about meetings, the term *balanced diet* is actually quite the opposite. As defined in health and nutritional dictionaries, the phrase means "a diet consisting of the proper quantities and proportions of foods needed to maintain health or growth."

Considering that the purpose of meetings is to keep your teams healthy and growing in the direction of their goals, it only makes sense that you hold the optimal number and type of meetings to achieve (and sustain) your desired level of team fitness and passion!

It's not uncommon to find companies or teams with overstuffed meeting calendars. Interestingly, the overeating analogy applies. Organizations that have too many meetings become sluggish and incapable of responding quickly to problems.

This was the problem at Carl's workplace. During a monthly committee meeting, it was determined that the procedure for a task Carl performed was to be changed. Because Carl knew the procedure inside and out, he sketched out the changes according to what they had wanted and handed them to the person chairing the meeting. But rather than accept Carl's input, the chair appointed Carl to sit on a review committee, which would meet for two or three days to determine the best solution.

Suffice it to say Carl that was not impressed, but being a good soldier, he went. Three days later, nothing was resolved and the review committee chair was upset. "I need something, people," he said, "we need a solution." Carl had heard enough. Once again he sketched out the solution, but he also took out another piece of paper and scribbled a few sentences. Then he got up and handed both papers to the chair. "What's this?" the chair asked. "One is the same solution I gave you four days ago. The other is my resignation. I quit."

In addition, just like overeating, some might humorously add that attending too many meetings is also a cause of indigestion.

At the opposite end of the spectrum we find companies and teams suffering from meeting starvation, and the health comparisons apply here, too. With insufficient or improperly held meetings, a team can stop functioning properly, often losing the strength to operate at its true capacity. In other words, a lack of information is like malnutrition to the corporate body.

How do we find a balance between meeting overdose and meeting starvation?

Unfortunately, the answer is "it depends." Just as people can have different nutritional requirements, the type and frequency of meetings you need depends on your team's personnel, your industry, the ever-changing economy, and where you are in a given business cycle.

But to help you determine your own healthy balance of meetings, let's look at why you have meetings in the first place. After all, your job as a team leader is to create the conditions for passions to emerge, and it's hard for people to get passionate about attending too many, too few, or unproductive meetings.

Meetings Must Have Purpose

As mentioned earlier, the general purpose of any meeting is to keep your team healthy and growing. This means your meetings should:

➤ keep people moving in the direction of company/ team goals.

➤ increase a team's efficiency and effectiveness.

However, each meeting also needs it own specific purpose.

As a team leader, you'll be attending meetings that other people schedule, but you'll also be a person who calls meetings for others to attend. Although you have little control over the meetings scheduled by others, you have plenty of control over the meetings called by you or by the people on your team, so let's make that our focus.

Whenever Heather receives a meeting request, she always wants to know what the purpose of the meeting is. After realizing one-third of her week was spent sitting in chairs, mostly watching PowerPoint presentations while someone read what was on the screen, she finally said "enough." She decided that her time had more value than that, and she was tired of wasting it.

Heather is a team leader of more than 18 people. Some on her team had already expressed similar feelings about wasting time at meetings, so one day Heather took a hard look at the different meetings she and her team were having. She chose the following rules for reducing meeting overkill:

1. Do not hold meetings if no clear purpose is stated.
2. Minimize status meetings.
3. For decision meetings, distribute information ahead of time when possible.

Let's look at each rule independently.

Do not hold meetings if no clear purpose is stated

Meetings become much more efficient and effective when they have a clear purpose and/or an agenda. The framework for any meeting is much easier to build when you're vitally aware of the specific reason you're holding the meeting. We can clarify the purpose of our meetings by answering one or both of these questions:

> ➤ At the end of this meeting, what decisions must I have in hand?

> ➤ What needs to be communicated?

We further strengthen the value of our meeting when we answer the following question:

> ➤ How does this meeting align with our team/ company goals?

Also, create an agenda for each meeting, and make sure each item identifies a person responsible for presenting or leading the discussion on that subject.

✗ Problem: People wanting to talk about non-agenda items

When someone has the authority to call and run a meeting, that person also has the authority to deny topics for conversation. Therefore, if you're running a meeting, you have the right to put all "new business" on the back burner until the agenda has been covered, or not even discuss the new item until the next meeting. The key is to do it respectfully.

This involves setting boundaries, and holding to them in a professional manner. People respect boundaries when they are enforced consistently and fairly, and when those who push or cross the boundaries are treated with respect.

Remember, the purpose of a meeting is to keep people moving toward healthy growth in the direction of team or company goals.

Minimize status meetings

With today's technology, there's little reason to hold most status meetings. The status of projects can be posted on a Website, sent via e-mail, or even posted on a physical bulletin board in the office. Many companies are now using online wikis and other Web 2.0 applications to track projects. The meetings section at *www.passiondriventeams.com* has a list of applications (with hotlinks) and other resources to help you notify people of status.

Know that when communicating status by means other than an actual meeting, potential obstacles exist that should be addressed. Common issues are listed below.

✗ Problem: Too much or not enough detail

When creating status updates, some people want to see a lot of detail and others don't. One idea that proves useful is to place a bullet point list of highlights near the top of a document. Then write a more detailed description that "fills in the blanks" for each bullet point, adding those paragraphs below, but appearing in the same order as the list. This method makes it easy for people to find more information on a specific topic if they want it.

✗ Problem: Team members not reading status updates

Sometimes people don't check the status of things that are important to the performance of their job. However, many online applications now include a "history" feature or document tracking log so you can check to see who has viewed what documents.

If you're distributing status updates using a paper-based method, tracking is still quite possible. Jack is a department head who created a sign-off sheet for each of his supervisors and their teams. Each person is supposed to read the status updates and sign off that they read it. Those sheets are due back in Jack's office on Thursdays, where his secretary compiles a list of who has and has not reviewed the status updates. That list is sent out to the supervisors the next day.

It didn't take long for peer pressure to kick in when people saw that accountability was genuine. And, to help build owner-ship and make things fun, Jack gives a prize to the team that has the best "read" record each month.

Even though it's low-tech, Jack's supervisors love this sys-tem. They say it keeps conversations flowing among the team members about what must be done next. And, nearly 100 percent of people in Jack's department read the weekly status updates.

✗ Problem: Misinterpretations

Whenever people communicate, the chance for misinter-pretation exists. This potential is multiplied when communica-tion occurs in writing. Solution for team leaders: Have the "occasional" face-to-face status meeting or teleconference.

Pamela oversees a team of 15 people at a distribution cen-ter in Texas. She says even though she posts various updates on the company's Intranet, she knows misunderstandings oc-cur. To keep things straight, she hosts an informal status meet-ing one morning each month. Pamela brings donuts and coffee, and it's the first thing that happens that day. To prevent this meeting from becoming a unidirectional data dump, Pamela keeps things fun and informal, and allows for dialog and questions.

For decision meetings, distribute information ahead of time

Heather chose this rule because she felt too much time was wasted presenting background on matters that required decisions. By sending out this information in advance, people can read it at times convenient to them. The benefits? People come to meetings already informed, plus they've have time to think about what issues they want to discuss. The result is often better decisions. However, Heather found out that when she sent out the material, she also needed to state clearly what decision was needed at the meeting.

But, like anything else, this time-saving practice has potential downsides.

✗ Problem: People not reading material ahead of time

The main issue here is whether people are prepared for the meeting. It would be one thing to not allow participation in a meeting by someone who did not read the preview material; however, that practice borders on micromanagement. On passion-driven teams, your team members are likely to have a good sense of responsibility, and will know whether they are sufficiently well-versed on a subject. Reading preview material may not provide them any additional information. Heather's rule was "come prepared for the meeting." If that means you needed to review the material, then she expected you to do so before the meeting.

The Value of Meetings

As much as some people would like to eliminate meetings altogether, meetings do provide value. Some meetings are like fresh fruit: They are refreshing and provide good nutritional value. Other meetings are like strange, exotic foods you don't like. They have nutritional value, but they're tough to swallow.

Still other meetings are like junk food. They provide no nutritional value and make you sick if you get too much of them. But many meetings are the everyday "meat and potatoes" variety. They may not be exciting, but they are necessary to keep you going.

Because you're the person responsible for the "health" of your team, you must learn which meetings are necessary for moving your team toward its goals. If certain meetings are found to have no value, cut them out of your team's diet. Meetings that having nothing to do with your team's mission, vision, values, or goals are suspect. You might want to toss them.

Each team is unique. A meeting that provides great benefit to one team may be poisonous to another. You must be in tune with your team's unique needs.

Sally, a nutritionist friend of mine, says whenever she counsels people experiencing health problems, she has them document what kind of food they're eating. Then she compares that record to when their health issues flare up, and often finds a correlation to a particular type of food. As you can imagine, when the patients refrain from eating the offending foods, their symptoms either disappear or are greatly reduced.

In the same way, you'll need to collect and analyze feedback about the meetings your team members attend to determine what your team needs more of, less of, or none of.

On the following page is a "recipe" for how to determine the value of your meetings. Consistent use of this recipe will reveal that adjustments and changes may be regular occurrences to maintain a healthy balance of meetings. Follow the recipe closely. And, for even better results, ask team members to oversee the data collection for certain meetings.

Continued use will also ensure that new team members become aware of each meeting's value.

Recipe for determining the value of your meetings

Ingredients needed:

➤ Data and feedback.

➤ Participation from your team members.

Directions: After each meeting, collect data and feedback on:

➤ The team's response to the meeting.

➤ The meeting's effect on the team.

➤ The meeting's impact on the vision, mission, values, or goal.

Note: "Impact on the goal" is measuring how much progress was made or how much movement occurred toward achieving the objective of each meeting.

You may also want to collect data on the appropriateness of the meeting's length.

➤ *Adjusting for attitudes:* When analyzing feedback, make adjustments for information provided by people who have perpetually rotten attitudes. Be careful not to confuse rotten attitudes with solid, constructive critique.

➤ *Analyze and serve:* Enter between three and 12 months' worth of data into a suitable word processing or spreadsheet tool. Call a meeting to analyze the data. After reaching consensus on the value, purpose, frequency, and recommended length for each meeting, re-arrange the team's meeting schedule as permissible so that it matches the results of your findings.

➤ *Yields:* A reasonable meeting schedule and a team engaged in knowing the value of its meetings.

Better results can be enjoyed when team members are asked to follow this recipe and oversee the data collection for certain meetings.

Consistent use of this recipe will reveal that adjustments and changes may be regular occurrences to maintain a healthy balance of meetings. Continued use will also ensure that new team members become aware of each meeting's value.

Four Basic "Food Groups" of Meetings

It's possible to take all the different types of meetings that occur in the workplace and categorize them into four basic groups. In *Death by Meeting*, Patrick Lencioni also identifies four types of meetings, and his book is very insightful as to why meetings work well and why they don't.

For the last section of this chapter, let's stay with our analogy and suggest that a balanced diet of meetings includes something from each of the following four groups.

Informational meetings

Status meetings fall into this category. So do presentations that explain what a company does or how a particular product or service will benefit you. Although usually led by one person, they can be interactive. Lencioni's "daily check-in" falls into this category—a five to 10 minute daily meeting to let others on your team know what's on your plate that day.

Because information meetings can be boring, it's best to keep them short and engaging. For example, Pamela in Texas brings donuts and coffee and keeps the atmosphere fun. To keep the daily check-in short, so that people stay engaged, Lencioni recommends that nobody sits down during the meeting.

This same approach is used by many restaurants. In what's known in the industry as an alley rally, restaurant managers meet with servers before a shift starts to review that night's specials, what wines would pair well with them, plus any other information to keep things operating at peak efficiency.

Problem-solving meetings

This type of meeting is more structured. It can include resolving disputes or crisis, identifying and removing obstacles that are slowing things down, and even project planning. Lencioni's "weekly tactical" meeting falls into this category. Problem-solving meetings address the issues of how to reach the team's strategic goals.

This type of meeting often includes sending out an agenda, although Lencioni's approach is not to create the agenda until after everyone in attendance gives a two-minute overview of their projects and what problems they're facing.

Typically, such meetings last one or two hours, although if the agenda is accomplished in less time, there's no compelling reason to stay. For example, Jerry heads up a small consulting firm in Southern California. On his way out the door to attend a meeting called by a customer to solve a production problem, Jerry told his secretary to expect him back in "two or three hours."

When Jerry walked back in 40 minutes later, his secretary asked if the meeting was cancelled. "No," said Jerry, "we simply resolved the problem right away. There's no reason to sit around and talk if we've already accomplished the purpose of the meeting."

Planning meetings

The purpose of planning meetings is making higher-level decisions. Such meetings often include plenty of constructive debate, analysis, and investigation into the issues. As such, the ideas that get generated at these meetings are often quite valuable.

Another way to think of the purpose for planning meetings is to answer the question, "What should we be doing and why should we be doing it?" Lencioni's "monthly strategic" meeting falls into this group. Whereas problem-solving meetings address the issues of how to reach a team's strategic goals, planning meetings are for creating those goals.

Retreats/teambuilding meetings

These meetings allow teams to step back from the action and refocus. For that reason, it's good if these meetings take place off site, away from e-mail and ringing phones. Questions that can be addressed about the team and its efforts include: What has worked well? What hasn't worked? Are people in the right place? Are we headed in the right direction? How are we working together as a team?

Lencioni's "quarterly off-site review" falls into this category. He recommends such meetings have light schedules, limited social activities, and keep their focus primarily on what's going on at work. However, many companies hold smaller-scale teambuilding meetings on a monthly basis, or even more frequently. The overarching purpose is to either achieve or sustain teams that are working together well.

For meetings that are off site and one or two days long, it's always a good idea to have at least part of the meeting facilitated by someone from outside the company.

Done right, retreats and teambuilding meetings help team members to get to know each other. This pays off on the job in the form of better communication, team cohesiveness, and a stronger commitment to team goals and objectives.

Summary

The purpose of meetings is to keep your teams healthy and growing in the direction of its goals.

Each meeting needs its own specific purpose.

We balance our diet of meetings better when we:

➤ Do not hold meetings if no clear purpose exists.

➤ Minimize status meetings.

➤ Distribute information ahead of time (when possible).

We can determine meeting value by collecting and analyzing feedback.

The four basic types of meetings are:

1. Information meetings.

2. Problem-solving meetings.

3. Planning meetings.

4. Retreats/teambuilding meetings.

Chapter 10

Listen, or This Won't Work

Jeremy was excited about his opportunity to make a difference. His new job involved a transfer to a wonderful city in the Southwest where he would serve as a process improvement specialist, analyzing projects and tasks, and making recommendations for increased efficiency.

Unfortunately, Jeremy found it odd that whenever he asked anyone for input on how to improve a project, all he got was an uncomfortable pause, usually followed by "I don't know."

The reason for this became clear at a staff meeting his second month on the job. The plant manager asked if anyone had thoughts on a particular capital improvement project. After a long silence, Jeremy offered a recommendation for how to shave a few days off the installation procedure—a move that would save the company a lot of money.

Surprisingly, the senior manager cut Jeremy off and discounted the data he'd presented. When Jeremy cautiously asked the reason, his boss lowered the boom by raising his voice. "I'm telling you, I don't agree with it, so we're not going to do it."

Suddenly, Jeremy knew why nobody offered input or made suggestions.

Poor Listening Costs Millions

Most of the time, studying communication involves attending speech classes and writing classes, but not many of us have been to classes on listening. That's a sad reality, because millions of dollars go down the drain each day as either a direct or indirect result of poor listening.

I have yet to conduct a class on listening and not have at least half the class say they already realize the importance of it and that they listen all the time. Yet when I give them a chance to prove themselves during an in-class exercise in which they demonstrate their ability to listen—everyone fails miserably on the first round.

The problem? Everyone wants to be heard first. And, if everyone is trying to be heard and understood, then nobody is truly trying to understand. When people don't feel heard they experience frustration, feelings of isolation, loss of team cohesion, and lower levels of commitment. If you're concerned about the bottom line, all of what I just mentioned leads to lower profits. In any case, I can guarantee you won't create a passion-driven team if you're not listening. It just doesn't happen.

The definition of listening

Hearing is one thing, listening is another. Before we continue, let's clarify what we mean by these two terms:

➤ Hearing: The act of perceiving a sound by ear.

➤ Listening: Truly trying to understand another person's point of view.

Hearing happens passively. As long as your ears are functioning as designed, you can hear. You don't have to think about it. Something happens that causes a noise, and if you're close enough, you hear it.

Listening requires an active, conscious choice. To listen, you must have a purpose in your heart and apply mental effort. Think of listening as a goal—an objective. A task you must accomplish.

Obstacles to true listening

The largest obstacle that inhibits listening is *fear*. People are afraid that if they set their own perspective aside for a moment and truly strive to understand another person's point of view, several things may happen:

a) It will be perceived as agreement, even if no agreement exists.

b) They'll learn something that shows their own perspective is incomplete.

c) They won't get a chance for their own point of view to be heard.

d) All of the above.

Because fears can be minimized when we have a plan, we'll look at listening in terms of two distinct steps, or skills. Conflict resolution, which builds upon these two basic skills for listening, will be covered in the next chapter.

Perhaps the most important thing to realize is that listening—truly trying to understand someone else's point of view—does not come naturally. Listening is both a purposeful activity, and it's a learned skill. Therefore, we have to work at it and practice it.

However, because bad habits or obstacles can prevent good listening, let's first take a moment to identify some of the more common ones that get in the way. If you see any of these obstacles within yourself, it would be advisable to work with your coach or mentor to find ways to eliminate them.

Seven deadly sins of (not) listening

Sin #1: Filtering. This is when a person's mind is sifting through the other person's words, looking for the lines where the Filterer and the speaker agree and disagree. Commonly, a Filterer nods when hearing agreement, but replies with "yeah, but ..." when hearing areas of disagreement. No effort is being made to truly understand the speaker; the Filterer is simply looking for where the two of them agree and disagree.

Sin #2: Second Guessing. People who are Second Guessing usually miss the real meaning of what someone is saying because they are too busy assuming someone has hidden motives and they're trying to figure out what those motives might be.

Sin #3: Discounting. This sin occurs when a listener lacks respect for a speaker. What the speaker is saying could be 100 percent correct, but a Discounter will either internally or publicly scoff at what's being said, using any number of reasons. The sad thing about Discounters is that they often miss genuine solutions to the problems before them, simply because they don't like the source.

A milder form of Discounting occurs when content is brushed aside just because the person speaking is not a good speaker.

Sin #4: Relating. A Relater is someone who continually finds references from his or her own background and compares them to what the speaker is saying. Severe Relaters often appear self-centered, because everything they hear is publicly compared or contrasted to his or her own experiences. A common phrase heard from Relaters is "That reminds me of when I...."

Sin #5: Rehearsing. This sin blocks much listening as the Rehearser is simply waiting for the speaker to finish talking, so the Rehearser can get on with what he or she wants to say. No true listening occurs when the Rehearser is thinking about his or her next sentence. Rehearsing is different from Filtering in that the speaker and the Rehearser may be in 100 percent agreement, but any words other than the Rehearser's own are just so much noise.

Sin #6: Forecasting. Someone who picks up an idea from a conversation and starts thinking about its future implication while ignoring the rest of the conversation is Forecasting. Forecasting can stem from being bored with the subject matter, or simply because one's mind automatically thinks ahead. One sign that someone is Forecasting is she suddenly change topics without any apparent logical transition. Although the Forecaster's ideas may eventually prove useful, the fact remains that no true listening occurred.

Sin #7: Placating. This is perhaps the most offensive of the listening sins. People who are Placating agree with everything you say on the outside, but internally they are not truly connected to the conversation. Possible reasons include: They don't want to take the time or invest the energy to listen, they don't really care, they're just trying to please you, or they're avoiding conflict. In any case, when Placating happens, you lose the richness of a two-way conversation. Placating is not to be confused with genuinely affirming someone. Placators are not really listening.

The mechanics of listening

You'll want to memorize the fact that listening requires an active, conscious choice. To truly listen, you must have a purpose and apply mental effort. You must genuinely strive to understand. Think about it: Without truly understanding another's point of view, differences of opinion cannot be ironed out, and trust cannot be established. Without trust, the conditions for developing passion all but disappear.

To build passion-driven teams, you need trust. Therefore, you must learn how to truly listen.

With this in mind, it's comforting to know that learning a few simple steps takes us miles ahead in terms of genuine listening and effective communication. But beware: These steps alone are only techniques. They will be effective only when based on a sincere desire to understand. The desire to listen must be born out of a realization that we don't have all the answers, that other perspectives bring value, and that if we don't consider different points of view, we aren't getting the entire picture.

Step 1: Focus on the other person

To truly listen, we must focus totally on the other person. This means putting your own opinions aside for a moment (no need to worry, we'll bring them back later). If something is distracting you, say to yourself, "I need to tune everything else out. I want to understand what this person is saying."

If that does not work, you can increase your focus by attempting to "see past the words." Do this by asking yourself the following two questions while the other person is talking:

1. What is this person feeling?
2. What is this person thinking about?

For example, what is this person feeling? Is he/she:

- Frustrated?
- Concerned?
- Thrilled?
- Happy?
- Disappointed?

What is this person thinking about? Is he/she:

◆ Identifying a problem?

◆ Describing a solution to problem?

◆ Expecting a particular action?

◆ Looking for help?

◆ Relaying information?

Don't be limited by what you see on these lists—they serve only as examples. The idea is that when truly focusing on another person, you're striving to understand more than the words; you're looking for the nuances, such as the thoughts and feelings surrounding their words. You're striving to see the same picture that's inside their head.

Step 2: Seek confirmation on what you understand

Step two exists to save you from acting on assumptions. You must seek confirmation on what you understand. Or, more accurately, on what you *think* you understand.

Up to this point, you may think you have a grasp on what's being communicated, but the other person has no way of knowing whether you do, and you don't either. Verify your observations and conclusions (which are simply "educated guesses" at this point) by seeking confirmation from the other person. This can be done several ways:

➤ Asking questions. *If I understand you correctly, you're concerned about the deadline for the safety reports?*

➤ Making statements, but with a voice tone that allows the other person to validate. *You sound really concerned about the safety reports.*

By seeking confirmation you allow the other person to say, "Yes, that's it," or, "No, not quite."

If you hear "No, not quite," ask the person to clarify what you didn't understand, and then seek confirmation after you've listened some more. Until you can summarize the other person's point of view, he or she will not believe that true listening occurred, and that will inhibit trust.

I cannot stress this enough. Until you can summarize the picture inside the other person's head, the other person has no way of confirming you understood.

It is quite possible that the process just described sounded extremely elementary to you as you read it, but I have observed no small number of senior executives who could not do this exercise face-to-face with a peer. It reads easy. It looks easy. But when the rubber meets the road, all sorts of obstacles get in the way. Do not be deceived by its simple appearance. Listening is one of the most difficult skills to learn, but these two steps provide the best method you'll find for confirming to other people that they've been heard.

When José, a senior manager, first learned this skill, he was skeptical. However, he saw an opportunity to try it one day when someone from his team, Janice, came into his office to complain about a coworker.

As Janice related the way her coworker was treating her, José paid close attention. Janice winced as she described some of the injustices. Her brow furrowed when she talked about what she wanted to do in response. Her voice was intense. Even though Janice hadn't noticed, José was totally tuned into her point of view. After she paused to collect her thoughts, José said, "You sound really hurt—even angry about this."

Janice looked up and her eyes grew as big as silver dollars. "Yes!" she proclaimed with amazement. The look on her face was as if José had just helped her solve a difficult puzzle. Then Jose watched as she sat back and let out a sigh of relief.

Out of that one conversation, José became a believer in first focusing totally on the other person. Getting confirmation on what we understand means paraphrasing what we hear. José did not repeat line-by-line what Janice said, he simply stated what he perceived to be Janice's feelings about the matter. Even though she was venting, she fully expected José to tell her "it'll all work out" or, worse yet, "I understand how you feel," when he really didn't.

The danger of "I understand"

A few common but erroneous phrases used by people are "I understand" and "I know how you feel." Because people are so unique, and have thoughts and emotions tied to so many different life experiences, there's no way we can truly understand how someone else feels. Saying "I understand" is a shortcut for not devoting the effort to truly see things from another person's point of view. As such, it shortchanges listening and the building of trust. The following story illustrates this point.

Bill was sitting with two of his coworkers on a Monday morning. The week before, he had been in charge of the company's trade show booth at a large convention. After Bill recounted some frustrating events from the week, one of his coworkers spoke up. "I know how you feel, Bill."

Bill froze for a moment. He realized what his coworker was trying to say, but it rang empty. Bill knew a lot of people who were at the convention and there was no way his coworker could possibly understand how some of those relationships affected Bill's frustrations. Bill didn't want to let it slide. He looked at his coworker and said, "No, you don't."

It's way too easy to say "I understand" or "I know how you feel." Don't shortchange your relationships and weaken your trust levels. When listening, everything rests on making a conscious choice to *truly* understand.

Listening is a prerequisite for building trust

Through the years I've seen many team leaders shoot themselves in the foot by not listening. The following is a scene I've seen in more meeting rooms than I'd like to remember.

Team leader Tom stands up to announce the particulars of an upcoming capital improvement project. After a brief overview, Tom gives what he calls a question and answer period.

"Any questions or concerns?"

Tom waits only five seconds before sitting down, saying, "Good. I hope to see everyone else as excited about this project as I am."

The problem? Tom's cutoff was too abrupt. Nobody felt he cared about what they had to say. As a result, their trust in Tom and their enthusiasm for the project were severely diminished.

Trust is also diminished when leaders don't seek input from their teams. For example, leaders at a large Midwest manufacturing company consistently left middle managers out of the loop in their planning meetings. This resulted in expensive problems that needed to be fixed after the plans were implemented on the shop floor.

The middle managers felt their input could have prevented many of these problems and saved the company much time and money. Unfortunately, they didn't feel trusted, and in return they lost trust in their leaders.

If you want people on your teams to be open and trusting, then you have to be open and trusting first. Time and again I've walked into businesses and seen team leaders walking around with their shields up. Their body language is sending the message of "don't talk to me." Like Klingon cruisers patrolling the neutral zone, their authoritarian and sometimes domineering attitude results in people giving them a wide berth.

People have good ideas. They want to be heard. But to capitalize on these ideas and build passion on teams, leaders must create conditions in which people feel safe to talk.

This requires that we turn away from the sins of not listening. We must turn off the filtering, second-guessing, discounting, relating, rehearsing, forecasting, and placating. If for no other reason than principle, we must strive to understand a person's words from his or her own experiences, not from our own. When people do not feel heard and understood, their trust levels remain low, and their passion has no place to soar.

Understanding is not a synonym for "agreement"

Note that "agreement" is not part of our two steps for listening. Yes, we must strive to understand, but this does not mean we must agree with what we're hearing. People can say things we don't believe, but when striving to create a passion-driven team, we must maintain the condition of trust, and that requires striving to understand someone, even if we don't agree.

When disagreements occur (and they will), your ability to listen accurately is essential. Listening skills are foundational to conflict resolution skills, which is covered in the next chapter.

Purposeful listening eliminates second-guessing and misunderstanding. But again—you must *want* to understand. With understanding you build trust and can move mountains. Without understanding, you're missing the mark, and diminishing the quality of your team.

The Top Five Reasons People Find It Difficult to Listen

In early 2009, the Center for Workplace Excellence, in cooperation with management-issues.com, conducted a survey to discover the most difficult situations for listening. The definition of listening was given as "truly trying to understand the other person," and the primary question was, "When do you find it most difficult to listen to others?" Here are the top five responses, in order:

1. When people drag on and on.
2. When I'm irritated with the person who's speaking.
3. When I've already made up my mind about what's being discussed.
4. When I'm distracted by other things.
5. When I'm not interested in what the other person is saying.

Listening is hard enough, and even more difficult when our motivation to do so is squelched by circumstances that irritate us. Yet being a skillful listener, even under stress, is necessary when striving to create passion-driven teams. Therefore, let's briefly explore ways to become better listeners in difficult situations.

People who "drag on" may do so for several reasons. One may be that they feel it's important to give abundant details, or it may be that they keep repeating certain facts because they don't think you've heard them. Still another reason for dragging on is simply a slower rate of speech.

Certainly more reasons exist, but the main point for listeners is that the other person wants to feel heard. By relying on the steps of good listening, you can break in (yes, politely interrupt) and summarize what the person is thinking and/or feeling.

This also gives you an opportunity to ask a question that redirects or refocuses the conversation.

Being irritated with someone or already having our minds made up about a subject also made the list. Patience and professionalism are what's needed in these difficult listening situations. Remember the phrase, "Acknowledgment does not equal agreement?" That truth applies here! In these conditions you can give yourself a reward for good listening, even when you don't feel like it.

For example, one client tells about attending a regular weekly event and having to "put up with" a colleague who rubbed him the wrong way. Rather than get flustered, he forced himself to listen attentively and show genuine interest in her never-ending boasting. He gave himself a point each time he did so, and after collecting 25 points, he would reward himself with a special drink or meal.

Being distracted by "more important things" will always make listening difficult. In these situations our brains are drawn to whatever subject holds more value for us. It's here that we may want to exercise our right to ask if a conversation can be held later. Acknowledge the fact that you realize it's important to the person and you want to give the matter your full attention, but "now is not a good time." The vital responsibility here is being sure to follow up and have that conversation later.

Finally, at times find we ourselves in a conversation that holds no interest for us at all. All the options we've explored are available for you: You can reschedule, you can choose patience and professionalism, or you can focus, summarize, and, if necessary, redirect the conversation.

Bottom line, listening is vital even in difficult situations. The level of trust you create depends heavily on your skills as a listener. Follow the steps for good listening and be proactive. Before you know it, listening won't seem so difficult.

If any of these apply to you, I strongly recommend thinking through how to deal with each situation in a healthy manner. Unless we listen well at work, a passion-driven team is just not going to happen. Therefore, let's consider how to become better listeners in each of these situations. The level of trust you create depends on it.

Summary

> ➤ Poor listening costs millions.

> ➤ Listening means truly trying to understand another person's point of view.

> ➤ Obstacles to listening include fear, filtering, second-guessing, discounting, relating, rehearsing, forecasting, and placating.

> ➤ The two steps of listening are:

> 1. Focus on the other person.

> 2. Seek confirmation of what you understand.

> ➤ "I understand" and "I know how you feel" are unproductive shortcuts.

> ➤ Listening is a prerequisite for building trust.

> ➤ Understanding someone does not mean you must agree.

Chapter 11

Resolve to Resolve All Conflict

On the outside chance you just arrived on planet Earth, here's an important news flash: People disagree about many things on a regular basis.

Okay, now that everyone is up to speed on that, let's talk about how to deal with disagreements, so we can have passion-driven teams. There are good ways and not-so-good ways to resolve conflict, but one thing is for sure: How we deal with disagreement and conflict either contributes to or takes away from a team's level of commitment and passion.

Before we get too far, some definitions are in order:

➤ **Disagreement:** A difference of opinion.

➤ **Tension:** A state of mental or emotional strain.

➤ **Conflict:** An open clash between two opposing forces.

The following story shows how these conditions can affect the workplace.

Stacy and Chris worked together on a marketing team that was trying to land a new client who is a manufacturer of high-end bicycles. Unfortunately, Stacy and Chris had differing opinions on how to sell themselves to the client.

Stacy wanted to promote the bikes as having the latest in cutting-edge technology, hoping to attract wealthy clients who like the latest gadgets and also have disposable income to spend on such bikes.

Chris wanted to promote the bikes as part of a fun, family-friendly activity as a way to sell multiple bikes and increase sales.

At this point, Stacy and Chris had a simple disagreement. However, that disagreement quickly turned into tension. When the team was holding meetings to iron out its proposal, Stacy and Chris started making snide comments and offhand remarks about each other's idea. Some of the digs became personal. That led to defensiveness and a near total breakdown in communication between the two. Before long, they were talking behind each other's backs, but hardly talking to each other face to face.

In no time at all, their strained relationship cast a dark cloud over their office to where people didn't even like coming to work anymore. This was tension on a grand scale.

Finally, the president of the marketing company said, "Enough is enough." He brought both Stacy and Chris into his office and locked the door. He said nobody was going anywhere until everything was talked through, no matter how long it took. During the next few hours, he facilitated an exchange between Stacy and Chris. It started out with blame and accusations, but as the president forced them to truly listen and consider each other's viewpoints, their loud voices subsided to a drawn out debate over the pros and cons of each idea. Eventually, they all agreed that the best approach would be to spend more time with the client and do some market research before deciding on the best path to follow.

"I'm glad we've learned how to have healthy conflict," said the president. "I don't want to experience that tension around here anymore. In the future, if you have a disagreement, please don't let it disintegrate into tension. Just debate it openly and honestly. We can have disagreements, so long as we debate them and settle on the best course of action for the company."

In healthy conflict all issues are on the table and discussed with objectivity. Each party can state his or her position with confidence that the other party is genuinely listening. That is, *wanting* to understand. Potential solutions are explored with open minds, with ripple effects considered and weighed for each solution offered.

It's an easy process to understand, but can be incredibly difficult to do if you don't have a plan. People want what they want, believe what they believe, and value what they value. So, if they don't see a plan that helps them get what they want, believe, and value, they won't hold much hope in finding a solution they'll like.

As a result, unresolved conflict is common. In some cases, one party just gives in. Other times both parties become stubborn and experience deadlock. Worse yet is when one or both parties become manipulative and begin sabotaging the opposition from behind the scenes, which does nothing but fuel more tension.

Which is better, conflict or tension?

In his book *Five Dysfunctions of a Team*, Patrick Lencioni explains how conflict can be good, but tension is almost always bad. Essentially, tension is unspoken conflict. Lencioni says people avoid conflict because they want to preserve a sense of harmony. The problem? Unspoken conflict causes tension. As we saw with Stacy and Chris, tension suppresses effective problem-solving, which happens to be essential for creating and sustaining a passion-driven teams.

Setting the Tone

Good listening prevents most tension from occurring. Disagreements get resolved quickly when we're truly understanding each other and seeking win/win solutions. But life happens. Deadlines can loom and clients can get upset. Family pressures can eat away at our thoughts throughout the day. A million things can contribute to increases in tension to unresolved conflict. When that happens, a dialogue can quickly dissolve into two monologues, with neither side listening to the other.

Whenever that happens it's time to open your mental tool box and start using the best tools you have for fixing whatever problems are besetting you. One of the best tools for resolving conflict has been dubbed "The Relationship Ladder" by my clients, because by following the steps, you remove tension and restore healthy working relationships.

The Relationship Ladder

Like any tool, you won't need the Relationship Ladder for every situation. However, the Ladder is an exceptional tool when the following conditions exist:

➤ When tensions are high.

➤ When conflict is unresolved.

➤ When the other person doesn't feel understood.

➤ When you don't feel understood.

In other words, if people are truly listening to each other and trust levels remain high, the Ladder can just stay in your tool box. However, if you encounter any of the four conditions listed, it's time to pull out your five-step Ladder and put it to work.

The following five steps serve as the "instruction manual" for this tool. You'll notice that the first two steps on the Ladder are the same two steps we use for effective listening. That's because true understanding is required for conflict resolution. Steps 1 and 2 are included here by way of review.

Step 1: Focus on the other person

People want to be heard and understood. The best and easiest way to do that is to focus totally on the other person's thoughts and feelings. Try in your heart to understand, and try to sum up the person's position in just a few words. If it helps you, try to imagine the same picture the other person is seeing in his or her own head.

Step 2: Seek confirmation on what you understand

Again, Step 2 saves you from acting on assumptions. When you seek confirmation on what you understand (based on what you observe in Step 1), other people can either verify that you understand ("Yes, that's it") or say, "No, not quite." If you don't quite understand their position, you can then ask them to clarify what you missed.

The purpose is twofold:

1. You need to understand the other person's perspective.
2. The other person needs to feel heard.

Keep in mind that during times of tension or conflict, the other people may express strong feelings about you. It's crucial you remain objective and follow the steps in order. If people do release pent-up anger at you, simply bite your tongue and seek confirmation that you understand their perspective. As the team leader, you cannot and must not take it personally.

Do NOT get defensive or you will add to the tension and make things worse. Step 2 is simply acknowledging what the other person is thinking or feeling. Just because you acknowledge someone's opinion doesn't mean you agree with it. Memorize the phrase "Acknowledgment does not equal agreement.

Step 3: Look for trust

People want to feel safe, so how you acknowledge their point of view is important. By using a non-judgmental approach when seeking confirmation that you understand them (Step 2), you're creating a safe environment. It's practically impossible to resolve conflict without trust, and the safer the environment you create, the more trust you are likely to generate.

Think of the presence of trust as the key that opens a gate to Step 4, because you're not likely to make much progress in Step 4 if you don't have trust.

By the way, your activity in this step is *look*, because it's not likely someone will come out and say "Gee, I'm beginning to trust you." You must look for it. Several signs of trust are relaxed body posture, slower breathing, and a lowered voice tone.

Step 4. Gently discover the truth

With trust in place, it's easier to reach the heart of a matter, the truth of what's going on. Your action word is *discover*, but be careful: the truth sometimes hurts. The truth might be hurtful to you, or to other people. So make sure you find it gently.

The "truth" of a situation might be:

➤ What needs to be done (sometimes by both parties).

➤ Why something cannot be done.

➤ What happened in the past to cause the present situation.

A good approach for gently getting to the truth is to ask questions, such as:

➤ What do you think really happened to cause this problem?

➤ What do you think could have happened differently?

Your tone of voice and facial expression must be free from blame or accusation. Be objective and inquisitive.

Also, if you've been biting your tongue and setting aside your perspective, it's here where you have the opportunity to present your side of the story. Just be sure to present your perspective in an objective manner. Make no personal digs and use an appropriate voice tone.

Also, be aware that the truth can raise emotions. If people get all fired up again after talking about the truth, you'll need to re-establish the foundation and start over from Step 1. Seriously.

Step 5. Establish hope

The first four steps on the Ladder involve the past. Step 5 moves us into the future, because in conflict resolution, establishing hope means finding a solution to a problem. This step works best if the solution is mutually agreed upon. It also helps if people discuss the benefits they'll receive when the solution is enacted.

The Relationship Ladder in Action

Joanne was listening to a manager from another department getting snippy with her over the phone. "What's wrong with you people?" he said, his voice rising in anger. "You pretty much do nothing all day long! All I'm asking is that you do your jobs. Why can't you get my simple request processed?"

As a new supervisor, Joanne was unaccustomed to such brash confrontations. But it was just this morning that this man's work request came in—and it was missing some vital paperwork. Moreover, other work had been flagged as higher priority.

To make matters worse, the manager on the other end of the phone was Mr. Jones. He had a lot of seniority, and he was famous for yelling without anyone challenging him. Getting on his bad side was not something Joanne really wanted to do.

Joanne knew this situation called for her using the Relationship Ladder. She didn't want to roll over, but she didn't want to be confrontational, either. She also knew she must maintain both a professional demeanor and a win/win attitude, and that both required careful thinking on her part.

Step 1 of the Ladder was to focus on Mr. Jones's thoughts and feelings, and Step 2 was to seek his confirmation. She also had to avoid his baits for an argument—his personal jabs.

She quickly reviewed what he'd said:

1. What's wrong with you people? (personal jab)
2. You pretty much do nothing all day long. (personal jab)
3. All I'm asking is that you do your jobs. (personal jab)
4. Why can't you get my simple request processed? (the real issue)

To acknowledge Mr. Jones, Joanne opted to seek confirmation on both his feelings and his thoughts. "Mr. Jones, you sound very concerned about this. To clarify, you're wanting to know how far along your request is in our system?"

Mr. Jones was taken back just a bit. Usually someone took his bait for an argument. "That's right," he said, a little off balance. He'd tried to sound gruff in his response, but Joanne thought she could sense his blood pressure drop even over the phone. "Step 3," she thought. "Look for trust."

Joanne decided to put a bit of time between Mr. Jones's anger and her response. She told him she would look into the matter and call him back. That gave her time to think through her response, and also time for his emotions to cool down.

When she called him back 10 minutes later, she double-checked to make sure he was relatively calm. Then she proceeded to explain her concern for his needs, but also remain firm on her department's policies. This was Step 4 of the Ladder: gently discover the truth.

Joanne conveyed the following to Mr. Jones:

> I see that your request is related to the ADA project and that it's an important component of your upcoming work. In looking at our schedule today, our workload has quite a few jobs flagged as high priority, which you may not have been aware of. All of our personnel are tied up on those projects this morning. But while I have you on the phone, I have your request here in front of me, and I notice some of the information is missing from the form. Can I get that from you now, or would you rather I talk with someone else about it?

She knew this was a fairly bold way to approach Mr. Jones, but she also knew that no magical phrasing exists. She just needed to remain politely firm on the needs of her department while also considering how she might get his request expedited.

Again, Mr. Jones was impressed with Joanne's professionalism. He wasn't thrilled that his paperwork hadn't been completed properly, but together they got everything worked out and his work request made it onto the schedule. This was Step 5.

Stick with the plan

It's extremely difficult to improvise when resolving conflict. If Joanne hadn't studied and practiced the Relationship Ladder, she might have easily bit on one of Mr. Jones's personal jabs. If she had done that, her working relationship with Mr. Jones would have been tainted for a long time.

It really works

Dennis also studied the Relationship Ladder. As a middle manager attending one of my training classes, Dennis put the Ladder to work when a disgruntled employee barged into his office all fired up and ready for a verbal shouting match. Instead of barking back, Dennis opened his mental tool box and pulled out his Relationship Ladder.

Dennis listened. He paraphrased. He restated. He clarified. He calmly acknowledged without judgment everything the employee had to say (even though he didn't agree with everything). Before long, the employee was sitting down and the two of them were having a regular conversation.

Then Dennis asked, "So, what would you like from me?" This was his way of establishing hope. His approach enabled the employee to focus on a solution to the problem. As they wrapped up, Dennis said he would look into the situation and work toward a resolution. And the employee left in a much better mood than when he entered.

Later, Dennis reported that same employee stopped him in the hallway weeks later and thanked Dennis again for handling his complaint so professionally.

These steps don't come naturally—you must make a conscious choice to follow them. But the five steps of the Relationship Ladder, used in order, give you a proven plan for resolving conflict. Remember, conflict is inevitable, but unresolved conflict demoralizes teams. Therefore, when creating passion-driven teams, you must confront and resolve all conflict.

Practice required

Recognize also that the Relationship Ladder is not a magic wand—at least not right away. You must practice to become proficient. But also realize that this five-step Relationship Ladder is a learnable system that does several things for you:

- ➤ It enables you to understand someone else's views.
- ➤ It enables you to demonstrate you care about the other person's view.
- ➤ It gives you a systematic approach to resolving conflict.
- ➤ It enables you to remain objective.
- ➤ It enables you to find solutions to problems.

All of these build trust—one of the necessary ingredients for creating and sustaining passion-driven teams.

An interactive lesson that allows you to practice the Relationship Ladder is available at *www.passiondriventeams.com*, along with other conflict resolution resources.

The bottom line is that every team has disagreements. How you resolve them can make or break the cohesiveness and camaraderie of a team.

Summary

➤ Disagreements can lead to tension if unresolved.

➤ Tension is unspoken conflict.

➤ The five steps of the Relationship Ladder are:

1. Focus on the other person.

2. Seek confirmation of what you understand.

3. Look for trust.

4. Gently discover the truth.

5. Establish hope.

➤ It really works, but practice is required.

Chapter 12

Poor Training: A Leading Cause of Trouble

The scene was a business lunch. Michael sighed heavily as he spelled out his frustrations. "I've been with this company for a year and I still don't know what I'm supposed to know. And from what it looks like, nobody is going to take the time to teach me."

Michael's natural sales ability helped him land a job in outside sales, but the industry and the products were new to him. He was scratching out a living, but he wasn't making the same money he'd earned elsewhere.

The reason for Michael's frustration became apparent when he described his training: two weeks of "shadowing" people in various positions within the company. No formal training. No learning objectives. Not even an outline of how to present and sell the product professionally.

"It felt like I was thrown to the wolves and asked to fend for myself," he said. "I think I'm going to look for work somewhere else."

Michael's situation is played out thousands of times each day around the world, because the overwhelming majority of managers and team leaders simply don't know how to train people.

Why People Leave

Research by Christian and Timbers found that the number one reason employees leave a job is boredom or lack of challenge. Reason number two is lack of opportunity for growth or advancement. In case you're wondering, "not enough pay" as a reason for leaving was way down the list at number nine.

Why so many managers don't believe this research is beyond me. What's really dumbfounding is that after 50 years of research, we find that employees' desires and managers' beliefs haven't changed. Managers consistently think workers want more pay. Employees consistently want a challenge and an opportunity for growth. One would think that with all that research, managers would finally get it. Alas, most don't.

Team leaders and managers must recognize that people on their teams want an opportunity to learn and grow, or they will have great difficulty creating passion-driven teams.

Counting the costs

Perhaps some additional research will provide some reasons to invest in good training.

A few years back, *BusinessWeek* published part of the Emerging Workforce Study. In it we learned that among employees who felt their company offered little, no, or poor training, 41 percent planned to leave within a year. But at companies where training opportunities were viewed as excellent, only 12 percent of the employees were considering work elsewhere.

That's a 240 percent greater chance of employees wanting to leave if training is nonexistent or viewed as poor! As they say, do the math. That's a lot of human and financial capital sneaking out the door if people don't feel a company is investing in them.

Just how much capital? Let's count the cost on that. How much does it cost to replace an employee who leaves? According to the Society for Human Resource Management, the cost of replacing an employee in the United States averages $17,000. Those making more than $60,000 per year will cost you more than $38,000 to replace.

If you want to invest in passion-driven teams, invest in training. The research is clear and consistent that employees want a challenge. Training challenges people to grow and learn new things.

Are you worried that you might train people and they'll leave? Remember that the number one reason people quit is because they're bored and without a challenge. When we do the math, we see that the costs of replacing people far outweigh the costs of improving their training. In other words, you can actually increase your training budget and save money because you're not replacing employees.

But more important than that, you will be engaging people who want a challenge and igniting their passion at the same time.

To illustrate how powerful training can be for your organization, let's consider how large of an impact training can have on a small company of 10 employees:

A. If a company of 10 employees with good training, on average, one person will leave (about 12 percent).

B. If training is poor or non-existent, on average, four people will leave (41 percent).

C. The net difference is three employees.

Now let's count the cost of losing those three employees due to poor or non-existent training. If they are "average" employees, the math looks like this: 3 × $17,000 = $51,000.

If they are salaried employees making more than $60,000, the math looks like this: $3 \times \$38,000 = \$114,000$.

Now take a look at your training budget. If you invested more in training, you would not only retain more people, you would save on all those hidden costs that eat up profits when you have to replace someone.

Considering the average training expenditure per employee is only $2,000 annually, most companies could double their training budget to improve the quality of their training and realize a huge savings, just from a reduction in turnover costs alone. And that doesn't even factor in the increase in productivity that comes from better-trained employees.

Getting back to team morale

Throughout this book we've been talking about intangibles to a certain degree, so let's leave the financials behind and just consider a person's attitude, or esprit de corps.

Think about the attitude that permeates a company at which 41 percent of the people are thinking of leaving. Compare that to a company where only 12 percent are thinking of leaving. Which group of people would you rather have on your team?

If we're serious at all about developing passion-driven teams, we need to ensure our teams are getting good training.

The Manager as Trainer

So far in this chapter we've looked at training costs, but let's stop and take a look at training methods. After all, one of the core responsibilities of managers and team leaders is training front-line employees.

Maybe you've been on the receiving end of on-the-job training. Perhaps someone showed you how to do something and then asked you to sign off that you learned the material. Never were your skills tested. No one asked you to demonstrate proficiency. You simply observed someone doing what you were supposed to learn, and they said you were "trained."

Unfortunately, this scenario is all too common. The problem? Such lecturing is not training. The ability to stand up and talk does not a trainer make.

In the same way, just because we show someone how to do something doesn't mean they've learned.

A couple of situations stand out vividly in my mind. One is the facial expression of the production manager for a large manufacturing plant. While conducting a train-the-trainer workshop, I reviewed what I call the "four step skill-transfer method." About half-way through the lesson this manager's eyes got big and his mouth opened. "So *that's* why our people aren't learning," he said.

Then there's the sales manager who takes a new sales rep out to show him the ropes. After meeting with a few prospective clients, the manager says to the new hire, "Okay, you've watched me do it, now it's your turn." Naturally, he's perplexed when his new hire messes things up. What's interesting is when he blames the new sales rep for "not getting it."

Don't misunderstand; this is not a criticism of these managers. If no one has ever shown them how to train effectively, then how could they possibly know? How adults learn is not a preprogrammed brain file, nor is it installed in us when we're born or when we become a manager. We must learn how to do it.

Therefore, the following is dedicated to managers and all who are responsible for teaching others how to do certain tasks. If it seems elementary, it is. The process can be tedious. It seems to take up a lot of time. But it also works, and works well. If you think about the time and money lost from people not performing tasks as they should, then this investment of time spent up front is infinitesimally small by comparison.

Why do I advocate this method? First because cognitive learning (knowledge/understanding) and physical skill learning (muscle movement/dexterity) are inherently different. This method separates the two, and puts brain learning before muscle learning. It's an effective order because when the brain understands what's supposed to be going on, it's easier for it to communicate accurate instructions to the muscles.

There are other reasons I like this method, but I think you'll see them as it's explained. Here are the four steps:

1. **Instructor Does, Instructor Explains.** This means that as the teacher, you must demonstrate what it is you want your students to do, and, as you're going through the various activities, provide narration to describe and explain what you're doing. As you demonstrate, explain nuances, tricks, tips, cautions, and so on.

2. **Instructor Does, Student Explains.** In Step 2, you're going to demonstrate again, but this time the student tells you what to do and what to watch out for. Be careful not to lead the student into any of the steps—he or she should tell you what to do before you do it.

   This step allows the learner to engage the new mental skill. He or she is seeing the procedure in his or her mind and is articulating it to you, but you have control over the actual process. A misstep in verbal instructions from the student does not have to be acted on if the actual doing might cause damage or harm. This allows for corrective instruction from you without damaging equipment or causing personal injury.

3. **Student Does, Instructor Explains.** In Step 3 the student performs the task with step-by-step instructions from you. Obviously, the student's mind is thinking about what needs to happen, but your instructions are providing accuracy and safety.

   Also in this step, one of the biggest obstacles to learning, student embarrassment, is kept to a minimum. The student can focus brainpower on the manual dexterity required instead of trying to remember what to do next.

4. **Student Does, Student Explains, Instructor Evaluates.** Here the student merges the mental and physical learning under the guidance of you, the experienced instructor. The student builds confidence and the stage is set for true ownership of his or her ability to do the task. It's not just "I showed you, now you do it." The student truly has the ability to explain what should be done and demonstrate proficiency in doing it.

This four-step method is not necessary or even applicable for all learning situations. But when teaching certain skills, it ensures solid learning. Again, it may seem simplistic, redundant, and time-consuming, but consider the options:

> ➤ Demonstrate once and then have to demonstrate again and again, plus fix all the mistakes later (not to mention lost productivity and profits).

> ➤ Take time up front so true learning occurs right from the start.

Give it a try. Yes, it takes time and patience, but the results pay you back many times over.

If you must design training

As I mentioned previously, the ability to stand up and talk does not a trainer make. Training is effective only if a learner learns—and that means trainers must know how to convey knowledge, skills, and/or attitudes in ways that people remember what was taught. For those who want to ensure good training, the following five steps should help.

Step 1: Analysis

Analysis, should be the first phase of every instructional effort. Typically, analysis begins with clearly identifying the gap between what is and what is wanted.

For example:

➤ What employees currently know versus what they need to know.

➤ What employees currently do versus what they need to do.

➤ What employees currently believe versus what they need to believe.

Note that analysis revolves around three areas: knowledge, skills, and attitudes.

For example, Michael's supervisor would have done a much better job if he had analyzed what Michael actually knew versus what Michael needed to know.

Step 2: Design

In the *design* phase we determine which learning objectives— what knowledge, skills, and/or attitudes need to be taught. For example, Michael's boss might have created one learning objective to be "explain the paperwork flow from order placement to product delivery."

Learning objectives should be based on specific duties and tasks related to the job, and are fairly easy to determine if we have conducted a thorough analysis.

Step 3: Development

In the *development* step we determine how an instructor will present material, accommodate interaction, allow for practice, test for proficiency, and remediate, if necessary. It's here that knowing the different ways people learn helps to develop effective training.

Step 4: Implementation

Implementation is the delivery of the training. Those conducting training need to create a safe learning environment and present material in ways that reach learners. The thing to remember is that if the learner doesn't remember the material, the trainer didn't do a very good job.

For Michael's situation, perhaps simulating answering customer questions with his sales manager would have boosted his knowledge base—and his confidence.

Step 5: Evaluation

Evaluation is determining the effectiveness of training. Some questions to ask:

➤ Were learning objectives met?
➤ Were the materials being used correctly?

For best results, evaluation should be an ongoing process, with any shortcomings addressed by making improvements to future training efforts.

These tried-and-true steps are used in education and training worldwide. To ignore effective training is to leave the door open for trouble. Learn more about how to create effective training at *www.passiondriventeams.com*.

The focus of this book is about building passion-driven teams, and training is a vital skill in that effort. It is difficult to get passionate about something you don't understand, let alone something you can't do. To ignore effective training is to leave the door open for trouble.

Summary

➤ Employees want opportunities to learn and grow.

➤ On average, in the United States, it costs $17,000 to replace an employee.

➤ Most managers have never been taught how to train.

➤ A systematic four-step training process can be used for teaching skills.

➤ A five-step systematic approach to training is used for designing any kind of training.

Chapter 13

Failure Is an Option

With all due respect to Gene Kranz's fine book about NASA (titled *Failure is Not an Option*) and the fact that in some cases it's truly not, most of the time, lack of success is bearable and should be considered a learning opportunity.

Sadly, people who "fail" are often castigated as losers who are to be shunned. What a tragic loss. What an initiative-killing, demoralizing choice. Every successful person I know has experienced failure. The same is true about even the best-run, fervently passionate teams. I'm told it was President Theodore Roosevelt who said, "Show me a man who doesn't make mistakes and I'll show you a man who doesn't do anything."

Most mistakes, oversights, and missed goals are not as serious as an oxygen tank exploding on a spacecraft. The majority of failures simply take us to a fork in the road, where we can either assign labels and blame or we can choose to learn.

Several lessons from history come to mind.

One is the oft-told story about inventor Thomas Edison. When asked about why he was failing in his efforts to create a lightbulb, he gave his now famous reply, "I have not failed. I've just found 10,000 ways that won't work."

Then there's Eddie Rickenbacker, who worked as a mechanic and laborer before becoming a flying ace in World War I. After surviving the war, he started the Rickenbacker Motor Company to produce automobiles, but the venture flopped. Later he started Florida Airways, but that flopped, too. Then, in 1938, Rickenbacker took the helm at Eastern Airlines, and turned it into the most successful airline of its day.

What if Rickenbacker had given up after his motor company failed?

Many have heard the story of Abraham Lincoln: Born to illiterate parents, Lincoln's first fianceé turned him down because she thought he would never amount to anything. After he did marry, three of his four children died before reaching adulthood. His business ventures failed, and he lost three out of four races for elected office before being asked to run for the presidency on the ticket of a newly established party. Yet many consider Abraham Lincoln to be one of our country's greatest presidents.

In each of these examples, people experienced tremendous failure. But instead of choosing to be victims, they chose to move forward. Allow me to emphasize something: Getting up and continuing to move forward is a choice.

Choosing victim status is the easy way out. When people choose victim status, there's no need to take responsibility. No learning occurs. The only result is a "poor me" attitude that puts a drain on the workplace rather than contributing to it.

If you want to create a passion-driven team, you must consistently help people up when they fall. You must not allow failure to become an obstacle to their future success.

Teach people that choosing to move ahead and learn from failure is commendable, productive, and, on a personal level, quite fulfilling. Naturally, it's not easy, but the return is much greater than the investment.

A now-retired acquaintance of mine, Paul Bremner, grew up in England. After a stint in the British army, Paul traveled to various countries, and along the way he learned how to manage a business. I was honored to make his acquaintance in Southern California. Paul's relaxed, successful demeanor and strikingly hearty laugh stand in stark contrast to the fact that he also experienced heart-wrenching failures along the way. "To hit rock bottom is devastating," Paul told me, "but you get up and you start moving again—wiser for it."

Again, the path to such an outlook is simply a matter of choice. The "self-talk" is different. The focus is different. It's forward, not backward.

Abraham Lincoln is quoted as saying, "I have simply tried to do what seemed best each day, as each day came."

Green Bay Packers coach Vince Lombardi once said, "The real glory is being knocked to your knees and then coming back. That's real glory. That's the essence of it."

The list of notables who survived failure and pushed ahead to success is long. Did you know Walt Disney's first cartoon company went bankrupt? Did you know best-selling author John Grisham's first novel was rejected by 12 different publishing houses? Did you know that Albert Einstein initially failed to get an academic position at the Swiss Polytechnic Institute?

Again, don't misunderstand; nobody says dealing with failure is easy. Getting past it includes facing fears. That was something Eddie Rickenbacker was well aware of. He said, "Courage is doing what you're afraid to do. There can be no courage unless you're scared."

How do you plan on responding when someone on your team encounters failure? Will you throw that person a pity party?

Will you stand next to that person as you both point fingers and blame others? Will you discredit and shun those people who "fail"? Or will you focus on growth and improvement, seek what can be learned, and move forward?

In the comedy *Cool Runnings*, an enjoyable fiction-based-on-fact movie about the first Jamaican bobsled team, the team's sled turns over on its side during the last part of the last race. After the sled finally skids to a stop and the team regains consciousness, they rise to their feet, pick up the sled, and carry it on their shoulders across the finish line. Even with their chance of winning a medal gone, they were still determined to finish the race.

Those who choose to focus on moving ahead are those who move ahead in life. Those who choose to focus on the negative are creating obstacles within their own minds that will prevent future attempts at achievement.

Realize that "stuff happens" and failure inevitably occurs. But also realize—and help your teams realize this, too—that you always, always, always have a choice.

Questions you can ask yourself whenever you experience a failure:

➤ What are the top five things I can learn from the failure of this effort?

➤ Who has succeeded before in what I am trying to do, and what can I learn from them?

➤ What can I add/change in my planning to increase my chances for success?

➤ How can I involve others to increase the number of eyes reviewing my progress?

Chapter 14

Celebrate Achievement

Ruth was at her microscope when Shawn walked up beside her, carrying a yellow piece of paper. "Here you go, Ruth," he said. "Somebody caught you at your best. Thanks for going the extra mile."

It took Ruth only a second to realize what Shawn meant. The laboratory at St. Luke's Regional Medical Center in Boise, Idaho, had recently started a "caught you at your best" program, which allows any employee to thank or acknowledge other employees for doing exceptional work.

On Ruth's card was a handwritten note, thanking her for staying after her normal shift and helping out in the chemistry department on a day they were shorthanded, but overloaded with work.

Ruth put the note in her lab coat pocket and almost suppressed the warm smile that crossed her face. "Someone noticed!" she thought to herself. It was a pleasant surprise.

Caught-you-at-your-best-type programs are being used in an increasing number of industries, and for good reason.

1. They provide specific detail about a praiseworthy behavior or attitude.
2. They're awarded soon after the praiseworthy activity occurred.
3. All employees are eligible to receive recognition.
4. All employees are empowered to give recognition.

In other words, it's nice when a manager notices you did something, but when coworkers notice and take time to write about their observations, it fosters esprit de corps—the spirit of a group that makes all the members of that group want to succeed.

The St. Luke's Laboratory Inter-Personal Relations (IPR) committee likes the program not only for these reasons, but because there's hardly any expense involved. The lab has nearly 180 employees, but running the program costs them only about $30 per month (each *caught you at your best* recipient also gets a candy bar put in his or her mailbox).

Employee recognition programs have their pros and cons. I'm a fan of *caught you at your best*, because it truly celebrates employees. Sadly, not all copmanies strive to do that.

How Do You Treat Your Employees?

Many companies proclaim that their employees are their greatest asset. Unfortunately, the phrase has become somewhat cliché, similar to saying employees are "empowered." These are valid statements only if companies put actions behind their claims.

In other words, if you say your employees are your greatest asset, do you treat them as if they are the most valuable part of your company? Do they receive the best of care?

If you're serious about creating passion-driven teams (and I'm assuming you are because you're this far along in the book), you must devote time and attention to creating environments in which the people on your teams can flourish. And when they flourish, you must take measures to ensure they are protected and well cared for, because that's what people do with their most celebrated and valuable assets.

If you were an art collector, your most celebrated and valuable assets might be a collection of paintings. Surely you wouldn't pile up your paintings or let them get rained on.

If you were a stamp collector, you would make sure your most celebrated and valuable stamps were stored and protected with extra care.

If you owned racehorses, you would ensure those celebrated and valuable assets were very well cared for, too.

I'm not saying treat the people on your teams as if they can't take care of themselves. I'm saying you need to protect your most celebrated and valuable assets and treat them well.

Protecting your assets

Amazingly, for all the hype some companies spout about how their employees are their most valuable assets, when you read articles and books about protecting business assets, never do they mention employees.

Granted, an asset can be defined many ways, but if employees are assets that provide a future economic benefit (and they are), it stands to reason that we ought to be finding ways to protect them. Yes, we can protect them with safety rules, with healthcare policies, and even with fiscal polices. Almost everybody does that, and everybody should. But if you're putting forth the effort to create passion-driven teams, then you're building a rare and therefore more valuable asset, so you'll need to provide a different type of protection.

This may not be what you were expecting from a chapter entitled "Celebrate Achievement," but I would suggest that by protecting your teams in the manner suggested below, you are also celebrating the fact that they've achieved something that few teams do.

After you've built your teams, the people on them will subscribe to common goals and values. They will coordinate their efforts to accomplish any goal set before them. Celebrate that ability, and protect it by not letting micromanagement creep into the picture. Always keep the team's values and principles part of the dialogue in your ongoing water cooler conversations.

After you've built your teams, the people on them will be concerned for each other's capabilities and personal growth. This won't be out of a desire for control, but their desire for camaraderie. As a result, they'll function as a cohesive yet flexible, interdependent unit. Celebrate that ability, and protect it by providing ongoing training, mentoring, and coaching.

After you've built your teams, the people on them will be adaptable, acquiring exchangeable skills from each other, both personally and professionally. Celebrate that ability, and protect it by equipping them with knowledge of each others' strengths and blind spots regarding their individual knowledge, skills, and attitudes.

After you've built your teams, the people on them will be highly responsible, seeking direction toward and connection to the team's mission. Their sense of common purpose will be strong, as will their desire to be seen as "can do" players. Celebrate that ability, and protect it by ensuring their meetings are aligned with the organizational mission and vision statements.

After you've built your teams, the people on them will share and receive information freely, including giving and getting constructive feedback. Such information will be viewed by the team as a supportive underpinning for their future success. Celebrate that ability, and protect it by continually modeling good listening skills, tolerating no divisive office politics, and practicing conflict resolution skills whenever you see potential conflict.

Are you getting the picture? Passion-driven teams grow. They emerge from many individuals into one team. And they become flexible but cohesive units when you create the optimal conditions for their growth and are vigilant in your guidance.

When that happens, they are very valuable. It only makes sense that you protect all that has emerged. Not by sheltering the people on your teams, but by tending the environment that allowed them to grow.

Get everyone celebrating achievement

Earlier I talked about *caught-you-at-your-best* programs, used by employees to recognize and even celebrate above-average effort and assistance from other employees. I promote the use of such programs because they encourage employees not only to recognize each other's strengths, but also to actively engage and look for value in each other.

When people on teams become highly supportive of one another, they develop a sense of oneness with a common concern for success. Celebrate that.

Celebrate when you see trust and when you see sharing. Celebrate camaraderie and commitment. And celebrate when you see common purpose and determined confidence. I believe you can do it. And, I believe that if you want to, you can create a successful, passion-driven team.

Appendix

Recommended Reading

Being successful in any venture involves learning. Although this book provides a solid set of principles and practices for building passion-driven teams, it cannot address every issue faced by team leaders. Therefore, please use the following list of recommended reading as a springboard for learning more. (Titles are listed alphabetically.)

100 Ways to Motivate Others: How Great Leaders Can Produce Insane Results Without Driving People Crazy
By Steve Chandler and Scott Richardson

It's hard to find a list of 100 ideas that are both practical and proven, but Chandler and Richardson provide such a list in this book. I like that they emphasize the need for personal responsibility in the leadership role, helping the reader see that "if there's a problem, I'm the problem." After all, without that foundational understanding, it's hard to create the conditions necessary for motivating people to move ahead.

You'll find this book easy to read, inspiring, and quite encouraging.

Boreout: Overcoming Workplace Demotivation
By Philippe Rothlin and Peter Werder

This book refers to numerous studies showing that an increasing number of workers are understretched, unmotivated, and immeasurably bored—and that the problem (what the authors call "Boreout") is more expensive, more widespread, and more damaging than the common malady burnout. They reveal common symptoms, phases of how the problem occurs, and how many pseudo-solutions do not help.

Interestingly, the heart of the problem is simply a lack of communication—from both employees and employers! After helping readers recognize the problem and its damaging ripple effects, Rothlin and Werder provide strategies for what people can do to turn things around.

Boundaries (When to Say YES, When to say NO, to Take Control of Your Life)
By Henry Cloud and John Townshend

Many people hesitate to set boundaries in their lives, because they're afraid it will cause people to dislike them. The unfortunate downside to that is when people don't set and maintain boundaries, others take advantage of them and often disrespect them. In my opinion, managers and team leaders must be very secure in their reasons for saying yes and no. Doing so based on a whim, and not principles, will destroy the environment needed to create passion-driven teams.

This excellent book is written by two Christian psychologists, so it contains a fair amount of biblical references. If that's not something that appeals to you, Manuel Smith's book, *When I Say No I Feel Guilty*, is a good alternative (also in this appendix).

Clear Technical Writing
By John A. Brogan

For anyone who must write, which is just about all of us, clarity is essential. Astronomical amounts of time and money are wasted due to confused and unclear communication. Sadly, and to make matters worse, an increasing number of professionals are churning out writing that wouldn't muster in English Comp 101.

Even if the writing you do is not technical, going through this self-paced workbook will sharpen your communications by showing you how to remove redundant and "puffy" words that make writing a burden to read.

Death by Meeting
By Patrick Lencioni

In my professional opinion, most meetings I witness or hear about are a colossal waste of time. It's likely that most of the waste would be trimmed if managers and leaders would follow the advice in this book.

It's a fast read, but don't expect a short synopsis. Lencioni has become a master in the genre of teaching through fables, and this book keeps with that genre. Although the fable itself isn't as riveting as some of his other work, the lessons in the fable on how to run meetings—and why—are second to none.

Lencioni explains why groupthink is dangerous and critical thinking is essential. He provides an extremely practical framework for how (and how often) to hold various types of meetings. Best of all, he stays generic enough so that any leadership team in any industry will gain from the principles he covers.

The Five Dysfunctions of a Team
By Patrick Lencioni

This book opens with a profound truth: "Teamwork remains the ultimate competitive advantage, because it is so powerful and so rare." That statement couldn't be more true.

It is my profound wish that *Creating Passion-Driven Teams* helps teamwork become more common, but I know obstacles to success will be everywhere. Identifying and getting past those obstacles is essential. Enter the aid of *Five Dysfunctions of a Team*.

Written in his fable format, Lencioni's *Five Dysfunctions* is as simple to understand as it is profound. The problems (dysfunctions) identified are:

➤ Lack of trust.

➤ Fear of conflict.

➤ Unwillingness to commit.

➤ Avoidance of accountability.

➤ Inattention to results.

Thankfully, the book counters each of these five problems with a solution. What I love about this book is it puts vital topics on the table for discussion—topics that are usually ignored or swept under the rug. I think this book has a huge impact on just about everyone who reads it. For an even bigger impact, have everyone on your team read it and talk about what your team can change to make things more effective.

High Altitude Leadership: What the World's Most Forbidding Peaks Teach Us About Success
By Don Schmincke and Chris Warner

Written by a management consultant (Schmincke) and a mountain climber (Warner—owner of a company that leads climbing expeditions), this book is full of analogies that are not only mesmerizing, but also very applicable to the workplace. The authors take the very real issues encountered while climbing mountains (such as fear, selfishness, arrogance, and lone heroism) and correlate them to what happens on leadership teams. The following pun is not intended, but this book is like a breath of fresh air when it comes to leadership books.

The Leadership Challenge
By James Kouzes and Barry Posner

Throughout the past few years it seems that every former high-profile CEO, ex-mayor, and ant farmer has put out a book on leadership. This begs the question, "How many leadership principles can there be that everyone feels obligated to write a 200–500 page volume on the subject?" My answer is, "Not that many."

With that as a background, I say we should have a trustworthy field guide, a solid overview of leadership principles that apply to every business and industry, and yes—even government. *The Leadership Challenge* is such a book. It's well-rounded, well-researched, and well-written. The "Five Practices" that form the outline are at the heart of all leadership:

1. Model the Way.
2. Inspire a Shared Vision.
3. Challenge the Process.
4. Enable Others to Act.
5. Encourage the Heart.

At first glance this book looks like a textbook. Don't be fooled, it's not. As I write this, *The Leadership Challenge* is in its fourth edition with 1.5 million copies sold. I think it's safe to say this is the type of leadership book that stands the test of time. I would suggest that long after the popularity of retired mayors, generals, and CEOs has waned and you see their leadership books in the bargain bin, you'll probably find *The Leadership Challenge* still on the shelf selling for its normal price.

Lessons on Leadership: The 7 Fundamental Management Skills for Leaders at All Levels
By Jack Stahl

In my opinion, too many books on leadership are theoretical, heady prose, filled with "I remember when" stories. This is not one of those books.

Although Stahl writes mainly from his experiences at Coca-Cola and Revlon, what he has to say is not just for executives of large companies. The material in this book applies to those in leadership at any organization—or those who want to be.

Lessons on Leadership provides compelling truths about the need for a focused strategy, measurable objectives, and communicating both of those with enthusiasm throughout the organization. Stahl also talks about information flow, reporting systems, and developing people around you who can help the organization achieve its goals.

I like the book because Stahl doesn't use corporate-speak; it's down-to-earth stuff. And he doesn't just tell us what to do. He tells us what questions we need to ask and why we need to ask them. Best of all he tells us these things based on a trainload of experience.

Living Toad Free: Removing Obstacles to Success
By Dan Bobinski and Dennis R. Rader

For those who would like to delve deeper into exploring the myths of motivation, this is a great resource. Dr. Rader was an educational psychology professor in my undergraduate program. I was doing a lot of management coaching at the time I took his class, and some of the material he was covering resonated with me regarding how I was coaching my clients to succeed. The concept for this book was born out of a simple story in which a toad represented an obstacle. Thankfully, when I approached Dr. Rader about collaborating on a book, he liked the idea.

The result is a collection of true stories from our clients, students, and colleagues about how people faced and dealth with obstacles in their paths (or failed to do so). The second half of the book provides more than a dozen "tools" the reader can use to minimize or eliminate obstacles in their life.

Presentation Zen: Simple Ideas on Presentation Design and Delivery
By Garr Reynolds

I first came across Reynolds's work by stumbling upon his Presentation Zen blog. For those who'd rather read a book than a blog, or for a quick reference to refresh your memory, this book is your ticket to creating more impact, more "WOW," and more audience connection in your presentations.

For those who give presentations, *Presentation Zen* shows you how to get your message across with dynamic, eye-catching techniques. In other words, you'll never be accused of delivering "death by PowerPoint" again. Even if your subject is technical research, it can be delivered with cutting-edge appeal. Reynolds shows you how.

The 7 Habits of Highly Effective People
By Stephen R. Covey

This long-time staple is on the list because I continue to meet people who haven't read it yet. Although I don't find this book as practical as other books on this list, I give it my highest endorsement. Why? Because the structural framework Covey provides creates a firm foundation for understanding how and why things work.

I especially like how Covey differentiates between leadership and management, between effectiveness and efficiency, and between "personality" and "character." The book covers a lot of territory, and the foundational material is often transformational.

Do not skim through this book. Study it. Absorb it. Teach it to others. You will find it provides you fresh insights each time you read it, and it will put your finger on some things you may have sensed for a long time, but could never define.

Six Disciplines for Excellence: Building Small Businesses That Learn, Lead, and Last
By Gary Harpst

Well-organized and easy to read, this is one of the most practical "how-to" books available for running a small business successfully and building one that lasts. In addition to sound advice, the book includes plenty of checklists, charts, graphs, and templates, making it easy to understand (and then apply) what Harpst is teaching. Consider this work a ready-made toolbox with what you need to know and do for building a solid business.

The six disciplines covered in this book are:
1. Decide what's important.
2. Set goals that lead.
3. Align systems.
4. Work the plan.
5. Innovate purposefully.
6. Step back.

This book is approximately 20 percent principles and 80 percent "how-to." Very practical.

Six Disciplines Execution Revolution: Solving the One Business Problem That Makes Solving All the Other Problems Easier
By Gary Harpst

If you are a business leader or if you run a business unit, you will be impressed with more of Gary Harpst's down-to-earth, practical, and very workable solutions. Using clear instructions with useful examples, Harpst shows that achieving excellence is not enough. Many companies reach what they define as excellence, only to fall out of it, usually floating back and forth between strategy and execution. Harpst explains how to avoid that common malady with step-by-step instructions for striking a balance to create *enduring* excellence.

As with Harpst's *Six Disciplines for Excellence* book, *Execution Revolution* contains well-thought out diagrams that help readers "see" what to do. Never have I seen step-by-step instructions for balanced execution explained so well as in this book.

Small Giants: Companies That Choose to Be Great Instead of Big
By Bo Burlingham

   In this book, Burlingham (an editor-at-large at Inc. magazine) identifies real issues faced by entrepreneurs, and I think he reaches out to them in a way that helps them value their role in the business community. Burlingham outlines 14 small businesses that focused on their passion instead of the almighty dollar, and yet gained huge profitability as a result. In other words, he shows us that growth for growth's sake is not necessarily the best route to wealth.

   Learn how to arrange your choices—they are many. Learn what it means to stay true to your vision and not succumb to growth for growth's sake. Learn the very real benefit of giving back. And learn to recognize the strengths and benefits you have as a small company that are unavailable to large corporations. If you own a small business, it's quite possible your teams will appreciate your focusing on the values described in this book.

Success! The Glenn Bland Method: How to Set Goals and Make Plans That Really Work
By Glenn Bland

   This inexpensive book has been around a long time. It changed my life in my early 20s, and I still refer to it today.

   Bland's ingredients for success include spiritual, financial, educational, and recreational balances. It's a spiritually based book on the subjects of self-starting and goal setting.

   Even a person who does not share the same Christian beliefs as Mr. Bland can learn volumes from his insight and wisdom in all the areas he covers. I especially like the importance Bland places on planning and organizing your day. In all these years it remains among the most practical advice I've ever read.

Taming the Abrasive Manager: How to End Unnecessary Roughness in the Workplace
By Laura Crawshaw, PhD

In recent years, the term *bully* has been used to describe overbearing managers who leave a trail of emotionally bruised and battered employees. Most people who manage this way are viewed as Climbers (described in Chapter 1). If you have been described as a Machiavellian, authoritarian climber, or if you have someone like this working in your organization, Crawshaw's book is a must read.

The reason? Abrasive managers don't see themselves as abrasive. They truly believe they are acting responsibly and for the well-being of their company. The bottom line is that they are simply relying on what's worked for them in the past, and they've not explored alternative methods that engage people rather than alienate them.

I've not found another book out there that approaches this subject as well as this one. Crawshaw explains what you can do, what you shouldn't do, and why. And her advice comes from real-world experience through years of work specializing as a coach to abrasive bosses.

True Leaders: How Exceptional CEOs and Presidents Make a Difference by Building People and Profits
By Bette Price and George Ritcheske

In this book (which is based on a nice piece of research), Price and Ritcheske identify principles for leading that are used by America's most respected and successful leaders. If you want to be the leader of a passion-driven team, these principles should become an essential "to-do" list. I can tell you from experience that less-successful and less-respected leaders seem to miss these principles.

Even though the book is a tad heavy with snippets of truth and illustrations from many different leaders, this is also one of its greatest strengths. In other words, when we see that such a large pool of thriving leaders are all saying the same thing, we begin to realize that what they're advocating must work.

Two Weeks to a Breakthrough: How to Zoom toward Your Goal in 14 Days or Less
By Lisa Haneberg

This book is based on the premise that people produce more breakthroughs and better results when they are both focused and doing something every day about their goals—what Haneberg calls "being in action."

The key to her program is what she calls "the daily practice." This is a combination of sharing your goal, taking action, and making requests, because these three things work together to improve both focus and action. Going way beyond theory, the book provides recommendations for how to keep the daily practice alive and well.

People often talk about what they're going to do "someday," but many of those great ideas never materialize because people get hung up in how and where to start. This step-by-step program takes all the guesswork out of moving ahead to achieve your goals.

When I Say No, I Feel Guilty Vol. II, For Managers and Executives
By Manuel J. Smith, PhD

As pointed out in the text of *Creating Passion-Driven Teams*, being assertive does not mean being aggressive. One does not have to be mean or intimidating to be assertive. In fact, quite often the opposite is true. This book does a fantastic job of delving into the nuts and bolts of resolving problems to everyone's satisfaction, and getting your needs known without walking on people—or letting them walk on you.

Essentially, this book puts a business focus on Smith's very popular assertiveness training. Many will enjoy the practical tips on handling the very real (and all-too-common) problem of coworkers trying to manipulate you. In fact, this is one of those books you may want to review every year or two as a refresher course for keeping your interpersonal skills sharp.

Why Don't You Want What I Want? How to Win Support for Your Ideas Without Hard Sell, Manipulation, or Power Plays
By Rick Maurer

This book does a great job of explaining how to do what so many do so poorly: *listen.* Then, building on the essential activity of listening, Maurer shows us how to work with others to create genuine buy-in for effective action.

Those accustomed to resistance and half-hearted efforts when implementing ideas will find this book insightful, practical, and truly helpful. Bonus: It's not fluff theory—it's genuine nuts and bolts.

Writing That Works
By Richard Andersen

Using humor and an easy-to-follow method, Andersen teaches us how to write. If you think you're a terrible writer, the method he teaches will give you tremendous confidence. If you think you're already a good writer, you will gain even more confidence. The core of this book describes the writing process in three stages: prewriting, writing, and rewriting. Andersen points out that most people try to do all three at once, and that's what trips up most writing efforts.

He also includes a style section, a mechanics section (just where are those commas and quotation marks supposed to go?), and a section for business writing. Most books on writing are rather dry, but Andersen's humor makes for an enjoyable read on what is usually a boring topic.

Index

achievement, celebrate, 193-197

adjust and asses, a need to, 35-36

adjusting based on feedback, 46, 47

agreement and understanding its synonym, 163

Airlines, Eastern, 190

assess and adjust,
a need to, 35-36
leaders, 48-49
managers, 42-44

assessment tools, 66

assets, protecting your, 195-197

attention density, 121-122

authoritarian leaders, 21

Behave, Different Ways People, 85-86

brain, human,117-118

builder or climber, are you a, 17-29

builders and climbers, 21, 22-25

bureaucratic leaders, 21

Business Case for Emotional Intelligence, The, 82

capabilities needed for success, other, 65-66

charismatic leaders, 21

climber or a builder, are you a, 17-29

coach,
get yourself a, 77-78
what to keep in mind when getting a, 77-78

coaches, 21

coaching, instituting, 67-69

comminicating ideas through organization, 46

About the Author

Dan Bobinski is president of Leadership Development, Inc., and director of the Center for Workplace Excellence. Dan was an early practitioner of coaching (he was the first management coach used by Qualcomm, Inc.), and his management development programs synthesize best practices in self-management, work management, and relationship management. These programs target managerial effectiveness, and achieve significant results. Dan's clients have reported a return on investment in the millions, and have seen the grievances drop by more than 60 percent. Dan has been providing management training and coaching to Fortune 500 businesses, as well as small and mid-sized businesses, since 1989.

In addition to being a dynamic public speaker, Dan is also a prolific writer on workplace issues. His Workplace Excellence blog (*www.workplace-excellence.com*) has been listed among the top 100 daily must-reads for entrepreneurs, and his newspaper column on workplace issues is syndicated internationally. Dan's writing has also appeared in *The Times* of London, *CXO* magazine, *My Business* magazine, *The Journal of the Institute of Management Services*, and hundreds of business newsletters, newspapers, and periodicals around the world.

A certified behavioral analyst, Dan holds a Master's Degree in human resource training and development from Idaho State University, and a Bachelor of Science degree in workforce education and development from Southern Illinois University, where he graduated Summa cum Laude. Dan is member of the American Society for Training and Development, the Society for Human Recourse Management, and also serves as adjunct faculty at Idaho State University. Dan lives in Boise, Idaho.